A History of Scandinavian Archaeology

Librill
de
Cimbris
et
Gothis.

OLE KLINDT-JENSEN

A History of
Scandinavian Archaeology

with 124 illustrations

THAMES AND HUDSON · LONDON

1 (*Frontispiece*) The early origins of Denmark are more favourably described in a Danish work by Nicolaus Petreius, *Cimbrorum et Gothorum origines . . .* (1695) than in the account by Johannes Magnus (see Ill. 2). The frontispiece shows the Goths, led by Gomer, son of Japhet, arriving in Denmark in the year 1800 after Adam, as indicated in the runes on the arches. The ark can be seen in the background, on a mountain-top, but some Danish prehistoric monuments are also shown: for instance, the row of stones beyond the outstretched arms of the two men may well be intended as a *dysse*. The female figure hovering overhead may represent Time or Fame.

Translated from the Danish
by G. Russell Poole

Printed and Bound in Great Britain by Jarrold and Sons Ltd, Norwich

Contents

Preface

The history of Scandinavian archaeology has its real beginning in 1818. For it was in that year that Christian Jürgensen Thomsen advanced his theory – based exclusively on the archaeological evidence – of the three prehistoric ages, Stone, Bronze and Iron, thereby casting light on that long and hitherto obscure period which preceded historical times and which Rasmus Nyerup described as having been 'enveloped in a dense fog'. That is not to deny that there were antiquaries before 1818 who made valuable contributions towards an understanding of Scandinavia's remote past, availing themselves not only of such antiquities as were then known and recognized but also of a literary tradition that embraced legal documents, reports, Icelandic manuscripts, and a variety of other recorded data.

The debt of gratitude I owe these earlier scholars I can only convey in retrospect; my indebtedness to the living who have helped me is evident from the source references. However, I must single out Professor Glyn Daniel, who has done so much to elucidate the history of archaeological studies in general and in particular to stimulate interest in the Scandinavian contribution, according it its rightful place in the context of European scholarship. I take this opportunity to thank him for his generous encouragement and support. I wish to express my thanks to the Scandinavian museum authorities for placing photographs at my disposal, and to those of my colleagues who helped me to find appropriate illustration material. I am grateful to Professor C.F. Meinander for reading the text with special regard to the Finnish aspect, to Mr Russell Poole for so ably rendering my Danish text into English, and to the Publisher for helping to bring this book – the first to devote itself to the history of Scandinavian archaeology – to fruition. For any errors of commission or omission it may contain I accept my share of responsibility.

OLE KLINDT-JENSEN
AARHUS 1974

RESEARCH into Scandinavian prehistory has been going on for four hundred years, but it is only over the last one hundred and fifty that it has been properly established. Up till then it was dependent to a greater extent than nowadays on talented amateurs and on prevailing fashions.

A unified treatment of research and conservation work throughout the Scandinavian world will be the most natural approach for this history, although full-scale collaboration was in fact rare, even in periods of political union. All the same, archaeologists followed each other's work closely and shared their findings. Moreover, not only was bringing the advantages enjoyed by archaeologists in any one Scandinavian country to public notice a useful method of improving conditions at home, but it also encouraged its neighbours to follow suit.

Though we must go back to the Viking Age in order to find a fairly homogeneous culture and language in the five countries, the tradition was kept alive, and archaeologists in particular were responsive to it. Even in 1688, in a period of tension between the two monarchies of Denmark-Norway and Sweden-Finland, the Swedish antiquarian Johan Hadorph, writing to his colleagues in Denmark, acknowledged this bond of sympathy.

Though the history of archaeological studies followed a different course from country to country, some important trends were shared by all. The convenient and frequent use of the word 'Nordic' to describe prehistoric monuments had its effect on their scientific study and on the museums. In the early nineteenth century two Danish collections were designated Det kgl. Museum for nordiske Oldsager (Royal Museum for Nordic Antiquities), and in Uppsala (Sweden) a similar name – Museet för nordiska fornsaker – is still used.

A constant rate of progress is not to be expected in these studies, given the national differences and the important role individual scholars have always played. If one were to go into the history of the subject in each country individually, the exchanges of ideas and critical comment would tend to be overlooked, and these are often of decisive importance. In a brief survey such as this it is more expedient to concentrate on the major figures and schools, even if it means omitting a number of details.

The present work closes with the generation before ours; there will only be a quick glance at the state of affairs today, for not only is it more difficult to view as a whole, but it is more closely bound up with the rest of the archaeological world than ever before. Even in the last century, when, for instance, Scandinavian archaeologists were studying European and oriental finds in an attempt to find connections, they conducted their discussions among themselves as a purely Nordic controversy. It is of little value, then, to study the discussions on chronology, typology, etc. except in relation to Scandinavian archaeology as a whole.

Even though political controversies in earlier centuries gave rise to polemics on the primary importance of each nation, friendly relations did exist, as can be seen for example in the letters of Ole Worm, Hadorph, C.J. Thomsen and B.E. Hildebrand. Antiquarians of different nations when seeking a responsive audience looked to each other rather than to their own countrymen. Indeed, some scholars did a substantial portion of their life's work outside their native land.

Archaeological projects and methods of training developed on similar lines throughout Scandinavia. Even so, each country had its own distinct traditions especially where legislation was concerned and in the form the institutions took. Some of these traditions reach back almost to the prehistoric period, others date from the Renaissance.

It is natural that this subject, which has not previously been treated as a unity, should be approached in somewhat tentative fashion. A number of monographs still need to be written before a properly balanced survey can be undertaken. Some important work has already been done, especially in Sweden, with H. Schück's thorough treatment of the early history of the Vitterhetsakademi (Academy of Literature) and B.E. Hildebrand's perceptive study of C.J. Thomsen's connections with other Scandinavian scholars. Useful sketches of the history of archaeology in Finland and Norway come from Tallgren, Nordman and Hougen. Among the Danish contributions there are notable studies and editions by T. Hindenburg, C.S. Petersen and V. Hermansen. References to literary sources are given in the bibliography.

Chapter One

Great Ancestors

ALTHOUGH it was only with the Renaissance that archaeology began its development, an interest in prehistoric remains was already taken in the Middle Ages. The great megalithic monuments and the treasures uncovered by chance or through tomb-robbing were its focus, but the reports and speculations of clerics to the effect that the oldest inhabitants of the North had originated from Biblical tribes also played their part.

Today buried objects of gold and silver are still being turned up through the working of agricultural land; such discoveries must have been even commoner in the past. Rich grave-goods were also to be found, particularly in the barrows, storehouses – so tradition had it – of legendary treasures from the distant past.

Modern investigations have shown that few of the large barrows escaped looting. It has been shown too that the plundering often occurred not long after the actual interment, that is while the grave-chamber was still intact. From the surviving grave-goods it can be seen that the robbers sometimes made off with substantial treasures, and this in spite of the dire threats invoked by runic inscriptions against would-be desecrators of the grave. Sinister tales also warned of mythical creatures who watched over the gold in the grave (as described in tales) and of ghosts – living dead – who could deal with presumptuous intruders. Possibly one object in tomb-breaking was to exterminate these ghosts.

Whatever the impact of all this on the criminally minded, it could not dispel entirely their urge for financial gain. Knowing, in all likelihood, the location of the grave and the position of the goods within it they went ahead with their ransacking undeterred.

The king, it is true, had further penalties in store for successful grave-robbers, provided they were apprehended. The old Germanic and Nordic laws decreed that any treasure which was discovered by chance and remained unclaimed went to the sovereign. This is expressly stated in the old provincial enactments, such as the Jutish law, codified in 1241: 'If any man should find gold or silver in a barrow or turned up by his plough or in any other way, it must be handed over to the king.'[1] The same provision, but ingeniously adapted to ensure recovery of the financial proceeds, was contained in the Swedish laws. From those of Östergötland it appears that two-thirds of the value of the find went to the king and one-third to the finder. On the other hand, the owner of the land where the treasure was found got nothing. A find at sea, such as a wreck, which presented the finder with greater difficulties, returned him a bigger share.[2]

Although (as we shall see) the Swedish law was later altered, the Danish law of treasure-trove or *danefæ* (literally 'dead man's property') has remained unchanged: it was incorporated as it stood into the Danish constitution of 1683 and is still valid in present-day law – an unbroken tradition from the early Middle Ages and perhaps from prehistoric times.

Those distinctive monuments known as dolmens and tumuli have impressed people ever since they were built, and with the passing of centuries stories grew up about them. The Danish chronicler Saxo Grammaticus was certainly not alone in contending (c. 1200) that 'in the far-distant past there lived giants, an ancient people to whose existence the massive roof-stones over dolmens and burial chambers bear ample witness. Should anyone doubt that these are the work of giants, let him say who else could have manoeuvred such enormous blocks of stone into position.' Whether giants or human beings of giant proportions were responsible was hotly disputed.[3]

Some of Saxo's theologically trained colleagues, however, found such explanations difficult to square with their Christian learning. They attempted to identify their oldest ancestors with the progeny of Noah: the northward movement of Japhet's people suited their case especially well. The author of the *Rydaarbog* (c. 1250) tells us that according to early historians the Danes originated in *Gothia*, and that the Goths themselves could trace their lineage back to Gog, a descendant of Japhet.[4] He may have known the learned tradition which held that the Goths were the people who had surged down from the extreme North (Ezekiel 38:14f.). He could have heard of this tradition from that widely consulted authority Isidore of Seville (d. AD 636), or even direct from Jordanes, who midway through the sixth century brought

2 Noah bids farewell to Magog, who is preparing for the journey that will eventually bring him to Sweden. Detail from the Coronation tapestry in Stockholm Palace (seventeenth century). The story comes from Johannes Magnus, *Historia de omnibus Gothorum Sveonumque regibus* (sixteenth century): after the Flood Noah settled in Scythia; his grandson Magog in AD 88 journeyed northwards with his tribe and settled in Sweden. A descendant of Magog, King Erik, gave the country its laws and deported part of the population to Denmark, where they were the original inhabitants. This mythical genealogy accounts for the names of the modern Swedish monarchs having such high pendant numbers

out a summary of Cassiodorus' fuller but now lost history of the Goths. When citations from Isidore crop up again and again in the medieval writers, this is no doubt because, as a cleric with considerable political acumen, and archbishop of Visigothic Spain, he was given to flattering the Gothic ruling class. In his discussion of the Goths, though no Goth himself, he stressed their exceptionally ancient origins and their immense strength and courage. The connection of the Goths with the people described in Ezekiel is one, however, which ultimately goes back to such authorities as Jerome and Augustine.

Later writers attempted to bring Biblical accounts into closer connection with the Scandinavian nations. Ingenious etymologies were propounded, for example, linking the Danes and the Dacians.

The Swedes, whose very provinces of Gotland, Östergötland and Västergötland seemed to echo the proud name of Goth, had most to gain from this approach. Jordanes' testimony that the Goths had come from Scandia added weight to Swedish claims of descent from these earliest champions of Christianity. At the Council of Basle in 1434 the bishop of Växiö, Nicolaus Ragvaldi, persuaded the impressive gathering that of right he should be seated in the front row as a mark of deference to his sovereign, the direct descendant of the Gothic royal house, whose power stood unrivalled even by that of Alexander the Great and whose distinction it was to have defended Christendom. He supported his contentions with an array of quotations from Classical authorities; and the sole dissident was a Spanish bishop who wanted the same seat himself in consideration of Spain's Visigothic past. Nicolaus gained his front-row position (though, admittedly, on the left-hand side) and then gave the seat next to him to the delegate from Denmark – a nice example of Nordic co-operation.

Nicolaus was not without imitators in this nationalistic brand of prehistory, with its assumptions of a Gothic heritage. The brothers Olaus and Johannes Magnus, living in exile in Rome, wrote proudly on Sweden's Gothic past, and one of their many avid readers was King Gustavus II Adolphus, whose ambitions to acquire international power were nurtured on books like these.

It ought to be stressed, however, that not all writers were seized by this mania for the Goths. In the 1530s the learned Swede Olavus Petri voiced a sharply critical point of view, denying outright that the Goths came from Sweden and maintaining that historians must base their arguments on reliable sources. As we shall see, Denmark too produced men who urged a sober appraisal of the tradition.

In these years prior to 1645, Scandinavia was divided into two 3
kingdoms: to the west, Denmark-Norway-Iceland-Holstein, to the east, Sweden-Finland. But frontiers were subject to change, partly as a result of war. In 1645 Gotland, which had belonged to Denmark for several centuries, was made over to Sweden; Skåne, Halland and Blekinge followed in 1658–9. The frontier of the Dano-Norwegian double monarchy extended as far as the Elbe. In 1814 Norway went over to the Swedish Crown, whereas 4
Iceland, Greenland and the Faeroes remained Danish; Finland came under the Russian tsar. In 1864 Denmark surrendered

3 Scandinavia around the year 1600. Denmark and Norway formed a twin monarchy, with Copenhagen as the capital, and incorporated Skåne (Scania), Halland, Blekinge and Gotland, which went over to Sweden in the middle of the seventeenth century. Finland and parts of the Baltic countries belonged to the Sweden of that time.

Schleswig-Holstein to Germany (and Austria), but in 1920 she recovered the northern part of Schleswig. Finland gained independence in 1918, Iceland in 1943, while the Faeroes and the Åland Islands now enjoy special status in association with Denmark and Finland respectively.

It is important to keep track of these changes, if only because they helped to determine which central museum should house the various finds; by and large, each part of the country had distinct traditions in archaeology, demanding a provincial museum to allow people to retain prehistoric finds in their own region as an illustration of the way their more distant ancestors lived.

4 Scandinavia immediately after the Peace of Vienna (1814). Under the provisions of the Peace Norway went over to the kings of Sweden, and Finland became a Russian grand duchy. Schleswig-Holstein, still Danish territory, extended as far south as the Elbe

Chapter Two

Renaissance Antiquaries

THE Renaissance stimulated this interest in antiquity. Italian humanistic enthusiasm for Classical culture had a parallel in Scandinavia, where scholars and statesmen, inspired by the past of their own countries, felt it their duty to inform themselves about the remote founders of the nations in question. Written sources and folk-songs were of course the obvious place to start, but inquiry expanded to include prehistoric monuments as well. This fascination with the national heritage and a reluctance to draw solely on the histories of other countries found vigorous expression in the North. For example, in 1581 the Danish historian Anders Sørensen Vedel spoke of how 'our venerable forefathers, the manly Cimbri of Jutland, the valiant Langobards, the intrepid Goths, the doughty Norwegians' deserved to be remembered for having defended the kingdom and for the achievements to which their lives were devoted.[5]

In the 1530s the Swedish historian Olavus Petri discussed the material available to him and assessed its value. An historian must base his work on sealed letters and similarly unimpeachable sources, like rune-stones and other inscriptions – in short, on tangible evidence and not simply on ancient records. He must be unbiased in his treatment of these sources. In dealing with the past Petri was careful to avoid allowing the political antagonisms between Sweden-Finland and Denmark-Norway to influence his judgment. How, he insisted, could one possibly decide whether the Swedes or the Danes were right when both claimed to have the older and more distinguished origin?[6]

His example was followed by others, like Vedel, who maintained that 'the life and soul of History is Truth',[7] though many of their contemporaries were all too readily provoked into making rash assertions that concerned their own age rather than the early age they were supposedly describing. Nevertheless, a sober objectivity was much favoured among Scandinavian students of antiquity. Documents were collected and monuments inspected, and the need to work from accurate drawings was recognized. This was the start of a formidable antiquarian project, which was to continue right through the seventeenth century.

As early as 1591 Henrik Rantzau, governor of Holstein, ordered an engraving of the field-monuments at Jelling to be made; the runic inscriptions were published on the same page, with a literal translation. Others soon set about copying and deciphering runic

5

5 View of Jelling, East Jutland in 1591, executed for Henrik Rantzau. It shows the two royal tumuli and the large rune-stone (B) *in situ*, with the runic inscription reproduced below

inscriptions, conducting excavations, and accumulating anti-quarian material. In 1588 the long dolmen known as the Langben Rises Høj, north of Roskilde, was excavated. Although the results were meagre – some urns and other unexciting finds – the scholars were not deterred from their search for evidence of the prehistoric inhabitants.[8] Above all else they hoped to find remains of the giant warriors described in folk-ballads.

Despite the mutually hostile policies pursued by the two double monarchies, it was recognized among antiquaries that the fore-fathers of each nation must have been closely related. The runes and language they were written in testified to that. Here was a field of research which could, and did, engage scholarly attention in both kingdoms. There was a spirit akin to rivalry in the examination and copying of these inscriptions, which in Sweden were so numerous that the antiquaries – industrious as they were – found it impossible to complete their work in the space of a few years only. The Danish and Norwegian archaeologists were better placed in this respect.

Such ambitious schemes could only flourish with royal support. Antiquarian research appealed strongly to the king of Sweden, Gustavus II Adolphus, in which he was influenced by his instructor, Johan Bure; the king of Denmark, Christian IV, evinced a similar interest for the ideas advanced by the energetic scholar Ole Worm, who was his personal physician. Johannes Bureus and Olaus Wormius (their names often appeared in latinized form) became leaders in their field. These men did pioneer work of formidable proportions, learning from each other at a distance and maintain-ing contact in spite of the tense political situation.

6
10

Resisting pressure on the part of Gustavus II Adolphus, Bure bided his time before attacking Worm's *Fasti Danici* of 1626, finally hitting out at the Danish scholar in 1644 in the poem *Runa redux*. Worm must bear his share of the blame, having contended that all Scandinavia was once under Danish rule and that the Danes enjoyed a generally more advanced level of culture than the Swedes and Norwegians. All the same, he tried to maintain an objective approach; taxed with having gone too far in depicting archaeological objects as Danish when they were actually Swedish, Worm was dignified in his reply: 'Among my things you will find nothing ascribed to the Danes except when supported by the testi-mony of reliable people or through personal inspection.'[9] One

6 Johan Bure (1568–1652) at the age of fifty-nine

7 Bure's drawing (*c.* 1594) of the rune-stone built into the portal of the Franciscan house at Stockholm

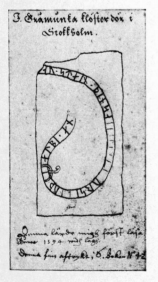

suspects that prodding both scholars there must have been bigots who wished their own native country to monopolize the grandeur of the past and who saw only a late reflection of it in the 'enemy'.

Johannes Thomae Agrivillensis Bureus, to give him his full latinized name, was the senior of the two Scandinavian archaeologists, having been born in 1568, twenty years before Worm.[10] He was the son of a priest in the Uppsala district, went to grammar school, but had a somewhat random education; he taught himself Hebrew and was for a time at the Franciscan college on Gråmunkeholm in Stockholm. He obtained a post in the Chancellery and in his later years was retained as a special civil servant, with a diversity of duties. In 1602 he became tutor to the young Gustavus Adolphus, later king of Sweden. Bure was exceptionally able and learned, and also unusually practical and clever with his hands; he was a good draughtsman and carved his own woodcuts for printing. The occult held a certain appeal for him, and one day in the year 1593 he noticed a rune-stone built into the portal of the Franciscan monastery. His interest aroused, he deciphered the inscription, having discovered in a book by Petri a table showing the runic characters side by side with their Roman equivalents. This spurred him on to further activity along these lines. He tracked down other rune-stones, did drawings of them, and in 1599 brought out a large folio-sized copper engraving showing ten rune-stones, nine from Uppland and one from Västmanland, together with nine inscriptions, one of which was from Rantzau's plate of Jelling; these he deciphered in a manner that could be readily understood. The careful engraving was again his own work. His newly earned reputation reached the ears of the king, Charles IX, who, on learning that Bure was contemplating a journey to Italy, remarked cordially: 'If you should die abroad antiquarian studies will come to a stop.'

In 1599 Bure got permission to travel round the Swedish provinces, and now began systematically collecting, drawing and studying with an eye to publishing the entire material. Having been able to engage assistants, he included forty-eight woodcuts in the book *Monumenta Sveo-Gothica Hactenus Exsculpta*. The illustrations in this book were painstakingly executed, and yet the first edition was a very limited one. The second and third impressions contained forty-nine woodcuts. Another publication he worked on but did not succeed in bringing out – the *Monumenta Runica* – contained copper engravings.

Antiquarian study had been initiated by objective methods. In 1628 the archbishop sent out a circular instructing the clergy to support Bure in his work. The inspiration for this came from Denmark, where in the meantime Worm had been making energetic progress; the Danish circular had been sent out some years before. Bure wanted information about rune-stones and early remains of all kinds. One pastor in particular, Martinus Aschaneus, submitted a very detailed report, but information poured in from other sources as well, underlining the need for a permanent institution to work on the material and to salvage the numerous easily damaged rarities – manuscripts, field-monuments and finds. In 1630, immediately before his expedition to

7

8

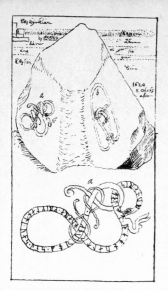

Pomerania, which plunged Sweden into the Thirty Years War, Gustavus II Adolphus established the royal antiquarian office (Riksantikvariat). This time Bure had stolen a march on Worm.

The king had great ambitions for Sweden as a European power, feeling that it must live up to the achievements of its early history; at his coronation he had mounted a tournament in which the ancient national heroes made their appearance. He insisted that the true origins of the Goths lay in Sweden, and that the present inhabitants were second to none in bravery, courage and loyalty. Now it was for the prehistorians to amplify and document these statements. He personally outlined a programme of work for 'Royal Antiquaries and Research Students of Ancient Remains'. The clear and rational objectives which they espoused at his bidding formed one component of his ambitious, not to say visionary, national policy. Antiquaries were to search for ancient monuments and collect prehistoric artifacts, such as might shed light on the Fatherland and in particular all old runic inscriptions, whether on stones or in manuscripts, complete or fragmentary. They were to scour all written sources, like chronicles and letters, to collect coins, and to seek out all vestiges of the ancient civilization of Sweden, so building up a storehouse of knowledge about the history of their native country. The king's high-flown pronouncement, that the Riksantikvariat must 'shed light on the Fatherland', would stand that body in good stead through bad times as well as good.

As Bure's assistants, two excellent research-workers were selected, Aschaneus, the pastor who had won commendation for his thorough report, and Johan Henrikson, Bure's future son-in-law, later to be ennobled as Axehielm in acknowledgment of the social standing of an antiquary.

These three scholars, professional antiquaries, went ahead energetically with their duties despite the magnitude of the undertaking. They journeyed all over the country, examining and describing altogether 663 rune-stones. Their drawings are astonishingly faithful to the originals, and the copper-plate reproduction is of a high standard. That there are divergencies from the

8 (a) Bure's drawing of a rune-stone in Ed, Uppland; (b) a modern photograph of the same stone

9 Woodcut of a rune-stone near Falebro, Uppland, from Bure's *Monumenta Sveo-Gothica Hactenus Exsculpta* (1624) (after E. Svärdström). Clearly and carefully executed, the forty-eight woodcuts in this book were only a preliminary sampling of a larger collection

modern interpretations is scarcely surprising: what matters is the attention to detail – which of course prolonged the task – and the understanding they showed for the general drift of the inscriptions even if, not unnaturally, there was uncertainty about the exact interpretation. All this work was to have appeared in a single publication, on which they laboured devotedly, but Bure's death in 1652 seems to have put an end to the plan. In 1648 advancing years and ill-health had already compelled him to give up working on the project, which George Stiernhielm took over.

By then, half of the rune-stones in Uppland had been studied, a quarter of the nearly three thousand in Sweden. This achievement, only one aspect of its work, clearly justified the establishment of the Riksantikvariat.

In Denmark-Norway the problems were similar and in no way diminished by the smaller number of rune-stones. Ole Worm, a gifted polymath, had taken up a career in medicine, ultimately attaining the important post of personal physician to the king; as a professor he was several times Rector of the University of Copenhagen. But his passion was collecting – archaeological and ethnographical specimens, naturalia, and much else pertaining to man's early history, natural history, and to foreign peoples. His greatest contribution, though, took the form of inquiries into prehistory, published in a series of imposing volumes.[11] Like Bure, he was Royal Antiquary in all but name; but Denmark's economy had been jeopardized by the unsuccessful wars Christian IV waged against Sweden in the years before his death in 1648, so that Worm's plans for a permanent antiquarian office on the Swedish model came to nothing.

10   Ole Worm was born in Aarhus in 1588. He attended the local grammar school, which possesses a fine portrait of him by Karel von Mander and also some of his student note-books. His studies soon took him to foreign schools and universities; on his return he went to the University of Copenhagen, where he was appointed Professor in Pedagogy in 1613; later he occupied successively the chairs of Greek, Physics and Medicine. He was a conscientious physician, and even during epidemics stayed behind to help while others were fleeing the city. This sense of duty was to prove fatal: in the plague of 1654 he caught the infection from one of his patients and died.

Worm's writings, especially his letters, tell us much about his personality. He carried on an extensive correspondence in Latin with the learned world of his time; he particularly valued his exchanges with Icelanders, who helped him with the Old Norse written tradition and discussed the interpretation of words in runic inscriptions. He was impulsive in matters that aroused his enthusiasm, ardently pursuing his own line of thought, but he also suffered periods of dejection for which the tense political situation and his personal troubles (he married three times) were mainly responsible. With Sir Henry Spelman of London he carried on an animated correspondence on such antiquarian matters as tumuli, runes, and the early origins of the aristocratic Thott family (which Worm traced back to AD 290, though Spelman expressed doubts).[12] He requested Danish ambassadors or private citizens

10 Ole Worm (1588–1654), aged 38. Engraving by Simon de Pas

travelling abroad to look out for Gothic monuments and inscriptions. His main aim, however, was to make an extensive search throughout the kingdom: with a view to correlating all the available prehistoric evidence, he arranged for a Royal Circular to be sent out instructing all clergy to submit a report in 1626 on any rune-stones, burial-sites, or other historical remains known in their parishes. To supplement this information, he dispatched

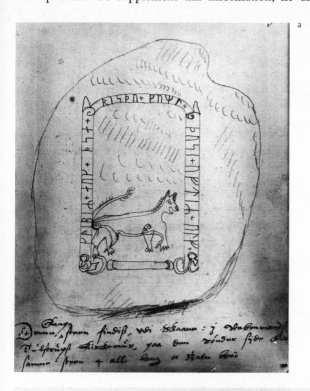

11 (a) Drawing of the Tullstorp rune-stone (Scania), made at Ole Worm's request by his diligent assistant Jon Skonvig, a Norwegian student who subsequently returned to his native country and became a pastor; (b) Worm's metal engraving from this drawing, in his *Monumenta Danica*; (c) a modern photograph of the same stone. The photograph shows how, in the early reproductions, the ornamentation was not rendered very closely, whereas the runic inscription, which chiefly interested Worm and his assistant, is copied correctly

draughtsmen to various parts of the kingdom; and here he had to rely on his collaborators. Most notable among these was the Norwegian theologian Skonvig, who prepared his drawings conscientiously, observing and transcribing the inscriptions accurately and supplying brief descriptions.[13] It was this mass of material which Worm used as the basis of his great opus on the Danish monuments, issued in six volumes in 1644, though it also took in earlier printed works. Worm's compilation became so authoritative that for many years there was no thought of revising it or of producing anything of like scope. Through his powerful connections and the interest in prehistoric monuments shown by influential personalities like the Chancellor, Worm managed to muster the resources and assistance for an antiquarian record covering the entire country. He kept firm control over the project and left bishops and pastors in no doubt that it had influential backing. A few samples of his correspondence will soon show the sort of conditions he worked under – meagre resources, eked out with almost uncanny shrewdness. The bishop of Stavanger could scarcely hesitate to act on a letter of February 1638 in which Worm opens by expressing sorrow over his wife's death and then goes on to furnish a list of monuments to be inspected, having first stressed that the bishop has promised to help, that the Chancellor is pressing for publication, and that Worm's correspondents abroad are urging him to speed up the work! The other bishops, he says, have done what was asked of them.

'It will be a light task for you if you get some young man (preferably a student with some ability in painting) to go the rounds of the deans and pastors with a letter of recommendation from yourself. Out of respect for you they themselves will be only too glad to look after his needs for the journey, including his provisions, and do all in their power to assist him. He should take a note of (1) the site, what county and parish it is in, (2) the orientation, eastwards, westwards, and so on, (3) the dimensions of the monument, its length, breadth, and thickness, (4) he should make a drawing showing the external appearance and structure of the monument, (5) he should add the interpretation he decides on, (6) local stories about the monument, even if fanciful, (7) noteworthy events in the vicinity, together with any other particulars that may be material to our investigations.'[14]

One of these assistants, a young theologian in Aarhus called Laurits Bording, is sent out with friendly encouragement to get good results from his antiquarian explorations, but Worm can also (in a letter of 1643) adopt a different manner:

'I am sending you a communication from the High Chancellor to the royal lieutenant in your county; he will be responsible for your transport and daily requirements during your inspection of the ancient monuments, and I feel certain you will ensure that there is no lack of enthusiasm on your part. I hear that there is a fine monument to king Hjarni on the island of Hjarnø; if you want to make the journey there, you will be able to find lodging with Ernst, the mayor of Horsens; he has promised you his help there.'[15]

In this way Worm recruited a staff of willing helpers, some of whom, through his good graces, were later presented with

12 Peter Alfsen, another of Worm's draughtsmen, copied rock engravings. This one was drawn in Bohuslän in 1627. He was uncertain whether the rock engravings were intended as monuments or merely represented the work of idle moments

13 An illustration in *Monumenta Danica* of ship-burials on the island of Hjarnø, Horsens fiord (probably Viking Age). The largest (A) is known as 'King Hjarni's grave'. The actual burials, still partly extant, correspond very closely to the drawings. The urns in the three corners were found on other sites. For no. 1 see Ill. 14; no. 2 was excavated by Worm in 1637 from a tumulus on the Kragerup estate of the Chancellor, Christian Friis; no. 3, which, along with no. 1, is still to be found in the National Museum, Copenhagen, was presented to Worm

ecclesiastical livings – Skonvig is an example. People came to know that it paid them to keep on the right side of this influential professor and royal physician.

The descriptions so obtained were incorporated into the great work on Danish monuments. In it discussions of rune-stones, barrows, megalithic tombs and much else can be found; there are maps of important localities like Lejre, where the residence of the earliest kings of Denmark was thought to have been situated. Inaccurate as some of the illustrations were – since Worm did not take as much part in preparing them as Bure – the result was none the less an impressive array of prehistoric monuments. At the same time he was much concerned with their preservation.

All Worm's lively imagination went into his study of the 'dysser', which we now recognize as megalithic tombs from the Late Stone Age. He was certainly correct in asserting, along with several of his contemporaries, that ancestor-worship was practised at these places, though it can hardly have been quite as this description would suggest:

13, 14

15

14 This late Bronze-Age urn (no. 1 in Ill. 13) was a prominent exhibit in Worm's Museum (see also Ill. 18). With the rest of the collection it was later transferred to the Royal *Kunstkammer* and is now kept in the National Museum. In his Latin note Stephanus Stephanius, a friend of Worm's, records that the urn was found at Vejrum and contained cremated bones: it was presented to him in 1649 by Mogens Høg, a member of the *Rigsråd*, and he in turn passed it on to Worm

15 Drawing of a *dysse* – megalithic grave – in Worm's *Monumenta Danica*, showing how – in his view – these monuments were originally designed: he supposed the stone slabs to have been placed on top of the mound as an altar but later, because of their great weight, to have sunk down into the earth fill

18

'They consist chiefly of earth piled up into a mound on whose top stand three mighty boulders, carrying a fourth one bigger, wider, and flatter than the others. Under this massive slab of stone a cavity can be seen. This cavity was presumably intended to receive the blood of animals slain in sacrifice. All over the country one finds altars of this and other types; the observant visitor may well find them impressive. But the gods who had their cult in these sinister places are worthy only of our contempt.'[16]

As a professor Worm obviously wished to avoid giving offence to the theological faculty, and his admiration for these imposing *dysser* is correspondingly toned down.

Detailed exploration and rune-decipherment were not Worm's strong point but he threw himself into the work whole-heartedly. Typical of the enthusiastic tone of his writings is his account of a visit to Tryggevaelde on 7 September 1624, when he examined the remarkable rune-stone now standing in the Rune Hall of the National Museum:

'First I removed all dust, dirt, and moss from the incised characters and marked them with chalk. Then I ran my fingers over the places where the characters were worn and difficult to make out and tried to distinguish them from cracks produced by weathering. Where I was still in doubt I consulted my companion who accompanied me, and so eventually arrived at this picture of the stone and the interpretation I have assigned to its inscription.[17]

The picture he provides is a good resemblance, but his interpretation has proved more problematic. Worm knew Old Danish and could read runes, but the lines of runes here have a special sequence. In a number of instances Worm's words and phrases correspond almost exactly to the present-day interpretation, in others they differ from it. The important thing, however, is that this Renaissance scholar approached the task in the correct manner.

Altogether Worm showed remarkable persistence and ingenuity in getting all he could from the resources available to him. He spared no effort, contributing from his own pocket when public support was not forthcoming. When his books appeared, he showed equal acumen in finding a market for them, sending copies to influential people and countering the critical reactions (often coloured by jealousy) which they evoked.

He adopted the same urgent tone towards prospective donors to his museum, making contact with travellers, sea-captains and landowners and writing to friends and acquaintances. To Rhode in Padua he wrote, 'Meanwhile, I beg of you, have posterity and opportunities of enriching my Cabinet of Naturalia at heart.'[18] When there was no alternative he acquired specimens by exchange. In this way his museum grew to be one of Copenhagen's most noteworthy attractions. We know what it looked like from the picture in *Museum Wormianum*, Worm's imposing catalogue, which came out immediately after his death in 1655. The eye is greeted by an assortment of the antique and the exotic: among the stuffed animals and bizarre skeletons is to be found a narwhal skull. (In this instance, Worm was correcting a misconception; ignorant of the appearance of this animal, people had previously supposed its tusks to be the horns of unicorns.)

The methods adopted in the arrangement of the museum differ somewhat from modern practice but have a logic of their own. The general classification 'stone' took in all types of stone object, including 'thunder-stones' or thunderbolts, a term often applied to stone axes. The *Museum Wormianum* contains the following description:

'Cerauniae, so called because they are thought to fall to earth in the lightning flash. They have various shapes, sometimes conical, sometimes hammer- or axe-shaped, and with a hole in the middle. Their origin is disputed; some deny they are meteorites, supposing from their resemblance to iron tools that they are really such tools transformed into stones. On the other hand, reliable witnesses state that they have observed these stones on the precise spot – in a house or a tree, and so on – where lightning had struck.'[19]

Worm had learned of this idea, with its Classical antecedents, from others; what he did was to borrow his illustration of 'flash-axes' from a Swiss work of a century earlier. Strangely enough, he failed to draw the obvious conclusion from the information he had been given on various stone objects now in his keeping. An Icelandic friend, for instance, had given him a harpoon-point which had been found embedded in a marine animal, commenting that it must be the broken-off tip of a fishing implement used in Greenland. He knew of New World stone tools and weapons, and had a drawing of three sword-shaped flint daggers from Mors. Similar pieces, with clear traces of human workmanship, were found in burial-mounds. 'We must conclude that the art of fashioning flint in this way has been lost, since it shatters at the slightest contact with iron.'[20] Worm was clearly puzzled.

A special upsurge of interest in prehistory attended the discovery of the first gold horn in 1639. Worm, with his unrivalled knowledge of runes and prehistoric remains, was subsequently given the opportunity to examine it. Here are his comments contained in a letter of 27 September 1640:

'A few days ago I was summoned to the palace at Nykøbing to attend His Most Gracious Highness the Crown Prince and others at the court, who were in poor health. Among other demonstrations of esteem and goodwill which were accorded me was the privilege of viewing a gold horn which had been found the previous year in Jutland. It was handed to me in the Prince's name, filled with wine, and I had to drain it. I marvelled at its construction – the precious metal of which it was made – but most of all at the wonderful grouping and composition of the pictures and hieroglyphs which decorated it. Everything about it points to the greatest age. There is no question that it merits some special study.'[21]

Worm himself undertook this study. By the next year, 1641, he had brought out the book *De aureo cornu*, one of whose most valuable features is the copper engraving of the horn, which is shown uncoiled. Regrettably, this and a second gold horn discovered about a century later were stolen from the royal collection in 1802 and destroyed. Worm's engraving is therefore of special importance. It will be understood that at that time it was possible to

16 The Tryggevaelde rune-stone, as illustrated in *Monumenta Danica*. In 1566 the stone was moved from Tryggevaelde to Vallø; in 1810 the Commission for Antiquities had it moved a second time, to join the collection in Holy Trinity Church, Copenhagen. Now in the National Museum

17 Worm's illustration of ceraunia, or thunder-stones. These objects are reproduced from an older Swiss work, though Worm had similar objects in his own collection

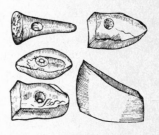

19

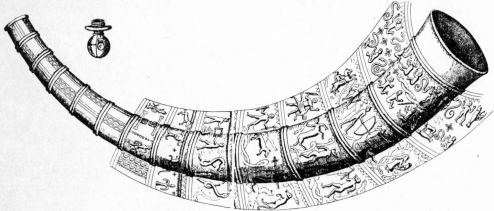

arrive at only a limited assessment of what the gold horn represented; the discussion centres around general points like the word 'horn' and its use, though the significance of the runes and pictures is also touched on.

On his death Worm's museum passed to King Frederik III. Installed in the old castle at Copenhagen, it lost none of its heterogeneity and romantic aura. However, the king, a man of scholarly tastes, planned a new building opposite the castle of Christiansborg for his collections and library. The second storey, which housed the museum, was not completed until after the king's death in 1680. It was open to the public on payment of an admission charge

20 The *Kunstkammer*, or Royal Collection, is on the second floor of this building which the king erected on Slotsholm, Copenhagen to house his museum; on the first floor is the Royal Library

21 Plan of the *Kunstkammer*, as set up *c.* 1682. The long Picture Gallery (1) connects with the Hall of Heroes (2), the Antiquities Room (3), the Indian Hall (4), the Cabinet of Artificial Objects (5) and the Cabinet of Natural Objects (6)

which went to the curator of the collection – the aforementioned *Kunstkammer*.[22]

Running the whole length of this second storey was a picture gallery some 80 yards long and 4 yards wide, which gave access to the five actual exhibition rooms, the Hall of Heroes, the Antiquities Room, the Indian Room and two rooms containing respectively naturalia and artifacts. A pair of spiral staircases led up to two antechambers which opened into the gallery: from there one entered the Hall of Heroes.

At the end of the seventeenth century there were some seventy-five prehistoric exhibits in the *Kunstkammer*; at that stage the gold horn was still kept in the palace. Three metal shields of Late Bronze Age type were regarded as foreign, though they had been part of a bog-find, and were hung outside. Moreover, flint objects were classed as 'ceruniae', or thunder-stones, and so placed in the Cabinet of Naturalia. A good forty adzes, axes, spear-points and daggers were shown with such vagaries of nature as conches and fossils.

The remainder, urns, bronze artifacts and the like, were on display in four cases in the Antiquities Room. They formed only a small fraction of the numerous curiosities dutifully published in 1696 in *Museum Regium*: there was the little anchor which had held King Christian V's ship securely at a critical hour, a 'fossilized' child, and a tree-stump in which a stag's antlers were firmly embedded. But one remarkable prehistoric find, at any rate, was to be seen, a gold bracteate which had been found by His Majesty himself in 1672 while on a September hunting expedition near Lake Esrom in north Zealand. No means of dating it were then known. It was published the following year in a medical journal by the famous physician and antiquarian Thomas Bartholin.[23] The runic inscription, a source of bafflement to present-day science, was translated into elegant Latin by a learned Icelander.

18 (*Opposite*)
The Museum Wormianum, a fascinating exhibition designed to stir the imagination and illumine various branches of science known to seventeenth-century savants. By the window can be seen one of Worm's treasures, the cranium of a narwhal, with its long twisted bony protuberance in place: it had been the custom to cut this off and sell it as a unicorn's horn, but with his acquisition of this cranium Worm was able to expose that particular fraud. Ethnographical exhibits rub shoulders with stuffed exotic animals, geological specimens and much else. Among the prehistoric exhibits can be seen the Vejrum urn (centre, fourth shelf from the bottom) shown in Ill. 14. The boxes marked 'lapides' and 'metalla' contained, respectively, flint and bronze objects

19 (*Opposite*)
The gold horn from Gallehus, south Jutland, discovered in 1639. Worm's illustration in his *De aureo cornu* (1641) shows the decoration on the horn as if spread out flat, and appears to be a faithful reproduction. The knob was added later while the horn was in the possession of the Hereditary Prince Christian

22 (a) Bracteate from Zealand, illustrated and discussed by Thomas Bartholin the Younger (after a picture in his father's publication of 1673) in *Antiqvitates Danicae* (1689); (b) bracteate from Vä, Scania, illustrated by H. Schefferus in his *De orbibus tribus aureis*, which, published in 1675, was the first work in Swedish on archaeological finds

23 Johan Hadorph (1630–97)

In his young days, Bartholin had spent many years studying abroad. In Padua he became friendly with the distinguished physician Licetius, who had published a book on ancient rings. Bartholin's study on arm-rings appeared in 1647, soon after his return home (*De armillis veterum, praesertim Danorum*). In its general plan it resembles Worm's monograph on the gold horn, devoting special attention to questions which would not concern a modern archaeologist. A good third of the text is made up of quotations, from Saxo to Snorri. The seven chapters treat of the etymology of the word, how arm-rings were worn, the materials they were made from, their shape and appearance, the fact that they were worn by both sexes, and their use amongst various peoples. Illustrated were two Danish finds from the *Kunstkammer*, a cylindrical Late Bronze Age arm-ring and a Viking-period ring-clasp: Bartholin was misled by the absence of the tongue on this clasp. The remaining commentary was chiefly on prehistoric ornaments.

The son, Thomas Bartholin, a history professor, inherited his father's interest in prehistory. Appointed Royal Antiquary in 1684, he was an assiduous collector and salvager of manuscripts. He had an invaluable assistant in the Icelander Arni Magnusson, who also helped with the work *Antiquitatum Danicarum de causis contemptae a Danis adhuc gentilibus mortis libri tres*, a three-volume essay on the cultural history of early Denmark, in which he attempted to explain, with reference to written sources as well as to 'anti-quities' properly so called, such as bracteates, rune-stones and some spears of more recent date, the scornful attitude of the heathen Danes towards death. In 1690, a year after his book was published, Bartholin died, and, unhappily, no replacement was ever found. The manuscript collection flourished, however, thanks to the capable Magnusson's continued journeys to Iceland; his bequest of manuscripts to Copenhagen University is in every way unique.

In Sweden antiquarian work fared better – though for a limited time only – thanks to a number of gifted individuals most promi-nent among whom was the Royal Chancellor Magnus Gabriel de la Gardie. He was able to do his work through the University of Uppsala, being Chancellor there as well: in 1662 a Chair of Antiquities was created and Olof Verelius became the first pro-fessor; in 1666 he was appointed Royal Antiquary. The same year, however, saw the creation of the Antiquities College, which being an affiliate body of Uppsala University, effectively brought the office of Royal Antiquary under University auspices.[24]

This scheme was put forward by the University Secretary, Johan Hadorph. An energetic, forthright type of man, Hadorph was at the same time shrewd and well-informed, active both as a historical researcher and as an administrator, and he worked in close co-operation with the Chancellor. He was supported in his scheme by Professor Olof Rudbeck, a far-sighted scholar who was to exert immense influence on the subsequent destiny of the College.

Hadorph was born and bred on an Östergötland farm which bore the family name, Hadorph. He began his studies at Uppsala in 1648 and in 1660 became Secretary to the Academy, as the

University was then known, holding this post until, in 1676, the affairs of the Antiquities College became his full-time concern. Influentially placed, he gained the title of professor in 1669 and was later appointed Secretarius Archivi, whereby he ranked higher than the Royal Antiquary. From there it was a natural step for him to be made an assessor in the Antiquities College in 1666, in company with four other professors. One of these was Verelius, the Royal Antiquary. The post of Director was given to Stiernhielm, and at Hadorph's insistence a complete staff of assistants was engaged.

The principles that were to govern the work of the College were sketched out by de la Gardie, along lines recommended by Hadorph. They were submitted to the Government on 14 November 1666 and received the royal assent a fortnight later. The preamble to this proclamation deplores the prevailing apathy toward ancient monuments: nothing was being done to prevent their decay and destruction – even such ruins as were left were being dispersed – and there was no recognition of their true worth as testimony to posterity of the 'heroic achievements of the kings of Sweden and Gotland, their subjects, and other great men – the imposing castles, fortresses, and dolmens, the stones bearing runic inscriptions, the tombs and ancestral barrows'. Henceforth it was forbidden to break up or interfere with these monuments, whether situated on Crown land or private property. Officials were to ensure that this prohibition was respected; priests and their assistants had the special duty of inspecting all field-monuments and sending drawings of them to the king.

This royal proclamation, the first law for the protection of monuments in the kingdom of Sweden and Finland, was accepted whole-heartedly by the provincial assemblies, and their approval was expressed in a resolution of the Riksdag (Parliament) two years later. Through it the Antiquities College gained recognition and was allotted specific duties.

A few years later this legislation on antiquities was extended by means of a further decree, made public on 5 July 1684; its purpose was to protect archaeological material 'found piecemeal in the ground, ancient coins of all varieties, and finds of gold, silver, and copper, metal vessels, and other rarities, many of which are at present being discovered and secretly hoarded'. All such finds had to be sent to the king, either directly or through the nearest district administration, whereupon the Crown would see to it that a reward was paid. Hadorph, who had also played a part in this important matter, had a rider added to the proclamation to the effect that the entire find should be surrendered in return for this reimbursement; up to then the legislators had kept to the old Swedish tenet that the find should be shared between the finder and the king. To the Antiquities College it was vital, of course, that 'such ancient and treasured things should be preserved, both for the glory of the nation and for the scientific interest', and should not suffer indiscriminate dispersal.

With these two royal pronouncements and with a college staffed by research scholars and their assistants, Sweden led the North in antiquarian work. But there was still need for consolida-

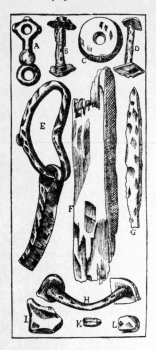

24 Hadorph's drawing of his finds at Birka, in the introduction to *Björkörätten* (1687). The objects, now in the State Historical Museum, Stockholm, are carefully reproduced. They are mostly ordinary iron objects, but include a rarer piece – part of a bit of English type made of bronze (A)

tion, and after the fall of de la Gardie from political leadership in 1680 and especially after the dispute with Rudbeck, the influence of the College waned. Yet, thanks to Hadorph's initiative and toil, its work continued to progress for a further twelve years.

Now, some of the assessors may have been less industrious than others, but they each took charge of some scholarly project – the editing of ancient laws, the historical study of the languages in Sweden and Gotland, and inspections of ancient burial-sites, fortifications, dwellings, rune-stones and so on. They studied coins, and their manuscript-collecting activities even took them to Norway and Iceland – then part of the double monarchy of Denmark and Norway – until Bartholin, the Royal Antiquary in Copenhagen, took steps to have this prohibited. Icelanders were engaged to study the manuscripts and to go on buying missions. The amount actually purchased, though not negligible, was small in comparison to the Danish collections, and the Icelandic buyers more than once gave occasion for concern; now and then they disappeared in Copenhagen and the Swedish Resident would be requested to track them down.

By 1675 the staff built up by Hadorph comprised an Icelandic scholar, two expert assistants who transcribed monastic documents and searched out antiquarian material, two draughtsmen, a clerk, a secretary, a printer, two men to prepare copper-plates and woodcuts in the printing shop, also a proof-reader, and a messenger and odd-job man. A clear sense of purpose can be seen in these appointments: research, preservation, publication – operations entailing substantial expenses, which were met by treasury grants. The Director and the assessors each received an honorarium of three hundred Swedish dollars over and above their actual salary, and the staff were paid an annual salary. The College was located in the Gustavianum, which now houses the Museum för nordiska fornsaker; here more and more material was steadily accumulated, and the College published its own books. Hadorph, for instance, brought out the laws of Björkö in 1687; in the introduction he describes his excavations in Björkö, which he justly identifies with Birka. The observations he made are sound and of importance even today. While trying to determine the position of the gates in the fortified city, he uncovered house-foundations and, just off the shoreline, a series of wooden posts, the remnants of a stockade which has now apparently disappeared.

Almost every year from 1664 onwards Hadorph went out on an antiquarian expedition, accompanied sometimes by a draughts-man or a writer, with a view to searching out and describing monuments. He found time to prepare reports and drawings of rune-stones and burial-mounds, and collected archaeological material, such as the splendid medieval treasure at Linköping church. Among his discoveries was the ancient paved road near Täby in Uppland, which is marked by standing stones, some with runic inscriptions. With publication in mind he wrote up all his observations and had woodcut illustrations prepared, but his plans failed to materialize. Some of the illustrations of rune-stones were incorporated in *Bautil*, which appeared in 1751.

In 1676 civil servants throughout the country were instructed to

25

search for ancient monuments in their districts and to send their lists in to the Antiquities College, which by now had enough work on its hands simply organizing the material.

A source of concern to Hadorph was the slowness in setting up a museum. The collection at the College was modest indeed compared with the Danish royal *Kunstkammer*, and so in 1673 – a time of growing tension between the two kingdoms – he made a journey to Copenhagen to see the royal collection himself. Unprejudiced in his outlook, he made a tour of all the special attractions, formed a friendship with Thomas Bartholin, his Danish counterpart, and with other scholars, and visited Roskilde, Ringsted and Sorø. But the *Kunstkammer* and the *Flateyjarbók* in the royal library made the most profound impression on him. He kept up this contact with Danish scholars, making no secret of the fact at home in Sweden: in a letter of 22 March 1688 he stressed their shared interests and the need for co-operation: 'I am of the opinion that we ought in no way to restrict the free communication of anything that may contribute to the anti-quities or the prestige of both realms, since we are one people, sharing a common language, even though we are ruled by different kings.' As late as 1691 he informed the Chancellery that he was corresponding with antiquaries in Denmark and getting them to send him books.

Hadorph did his best to cope with all the problems that beset him. Among the additions to his museum were three bracteates, on which one of the assessors, Professor Schefferus, published an interesting article in 1675. They had been found in Vä in Skåne, which province had in 1670 yielded a bronze sword, the first pre-historic artifact to reach the museum. But his work was threatened unexpectedly; for Rudbeck, originally a supporter of the College, had fallen out with several of the assessors. This was a consequence not so much of Rudbeck's ideas, to which they subscribed only in part, as of a number of practical problems. In the event, their new-found enemy was to prove more than a match for them.

Rudbeck was born in Västerås in 1630, and as early as 1653 was appointed to a professorship at the University of Uppsala. Having served as Rector, and being an influential member of the Con-

26 Olof Rudbeck (1630–1702)

sistory, or governing body of the University, he enjoyed both power and prestige as medical scientist and University administrator. But he had a gift for making enemies, too. He had laid out a botanical garden and built a well-designed anatomy theatre above 27 the Gustavianum. Suddenly he renounced nearly all these activities, turning all his energies to the study of prehistory. Following the example of Verelius, he concentrated on place-names and prehistoric remains, and all at once he was struck by the notion that the Swedish place-names were identical with Classical ones. He concluded that Sweden was really the vanished Atlantis, said by Plato to have been engulfed beneath the ocean. Since all the various ethnic cultures had originated in Atlantis, it followed that Sweden was the true focal point of all culture. Runes, Goths, the exploits of early history – all were elements in this fantasy. Worm's ideas of a Danish dominance paled in comparison. Rudbeck's own excavations appeared to supply him with further proof. It is worth examining the way he handles these observations, since it reveals both his strength and weakness.

His approach to the investigation of burial-sites is the rational one we should expect of a trained scientist and surgeon. He cut a 28 trench through barrows in Old Uppsala and drew the vertical sections, noting the characteristics of each layer and comparing them; in this way he was able to distinguish the ages of the burials. These were the first profile sketches to be prepared as part of an archaeological survey, and although there were few finds, the method was a sound one. At other sites, like Ultuna, he found iron nails from boat-burials, urns and so on.

Up to this point Rudbeck had done excellent work, but his volatile temperament now demanded a broader basis for his speculative theories. He designed a measuring-rod which would determine the age of each stratum from its thickness. In the first volume of *Atlantica* he explains the technique carefully: 'Now

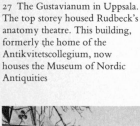

27 The Gustavianum in Uppsala. The top storey housed Rudbeck's anatomy theatre. This building, formerly the home of the Antikvitetscollegium, now houses the Museum of Nordic Antiquities

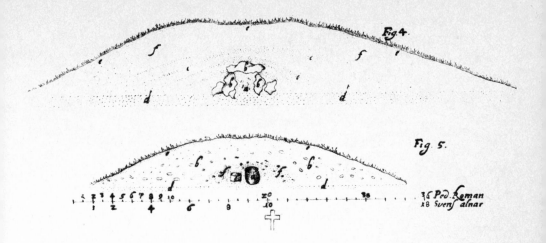

28 Rudbeck's drawing of two tumuli at Old Uppsala. It shows the vertical sections made as part of his excavation (from his *Atlantica*)

since some four thousand years have elapsed from the time of Noah's flood down to the present day, and during that period the total soil-cover accumulating on the earth's surface . . . has not risen more than eight or nine inches, I have accordingly devised a measure divided into tenths, and this measure I have used constantly: it is so graduated that a fifth part corresponds to a thousand years and tenth to five hundred years.' He believed, in other words, that measuring the depth of the soil above a burial-site would indicate to the nearest century the time that had passed since its inception. Clearly, he had by now progressed from his sensible initial observations and attempts at interpretation into the world of fantasy.

This remarkable man, part scholar, part dreamer, gained world renown, but his influence proved fatal to the Antiquities College, which did not hold with his ideas. In 1692 orders were given for its transfer to Stockholm and for its name to be changed to 'Antiquities Archive'. Whereas the word 'College' had implied initiative and enterprise, the new title, 'Archive', implied a more passive way of life on the part of its workers. Dominated as they were by the visionary Rudbeck, the College's industrious staff could find no one of sufficient authority to espouse their cause. The heady days of prestige and power were fast running out, and the following year, 1693, Hadorph died.

Nevertheless, a solid basis now existed in Sweden for a permanent institution, one which stood to gain by the law protecting ancient monuments and the compulsory handing-in of all finds. Antiquarian work was recognized as a State responsibility.

In Denmark-Norway such an institution was still lacking, though progress had been made in antiquarian work. Worm and Bartholin made their brilliant contributions but scholarship in this field, being entirely dependent on the energy and foresight of individuals, took on a haphazard quality after their death. The law regarding treasure-trove was a purely fiscal measure and could be applied to archaeological finds only insofar as they were of precious metal; nor was any conservation law passed, though Danish prehistoric monuments were even more vulnerable to destruction than those in Sweden.

Chapter Three

New Developments in the Age of Enlightenment

The dreams of international power cherished by the Scandinavian realms during the Renaissance were to evaporate in an atmosphere of economic decline, realism and scholarly debate. The aura surrounding that remote period of national greatness also faded away.

In point of fact the need to save threatened prehistoric monuments or at any rate to study them grew more urgent. The price of agricultural land soared in the eighteenth century. Land-speculators broke up the large estates and industrious peasants began working previously uncultivated land. From 1750 onwards, and especially in southern Scandinavia, this changed pattern of land-use had drastic effects on tumuli and burial-chambers. Road-builders were free to cart away the stones where these were conveniently available. The antiquarian institutions, for their part, were not vigorous enough to put a stop to this unfortunate state of affairs, although the headmaster at Odense, Thomas Bircherod, drew attention to the seriousness of the situation and there were others engaged on research who tried to salvage what they could. Ludvig Holberg, the Dano-Norwegian scholar and comedy-writer, hints at these exceptions to the general indifference in his sardonic way: 'studying Nordic antiquities is like scrabbling in dung-hills: it is an occupation to which certain people might well be sentenced for their crimes, if there were not already so many keen amateurs in the field!'[25]

Nevertheless archaeology still had a wide following. It featured among the subjects that were studied in the learned academies founded about the middle of the eighteenth century. The Danish Royal Society, for instance, published a paper on archaeological excavations in the first (1744) issue of its periodical. In 1753 the queen of Sweden, Lovisa Ulrika, Frederick the Great's sister, founded the Vitterhetsakademi, whose objectives were the study of history, antiquities and rhetoric. In Norway the Norwegian Royal Society, founded in Trondheim in 1760, was active in archaeology, conducting excavations and setting up a museum. So it came about that archaeology was cultivated by scholars who not only worked from written sources but from observations of finds and artifacts. This was of the utmost significance for the future course of the discipline.

A further step was taken when scholars pointed out the resemblance between the way of life of primitive peoples from other parts of the world and that of the prehistoric inhabitants of

Scandinavia. On the other hand, we shall see how material from the Bible and the chronicles continued to be pressed into service to supply a 'history' for the long period which lay outside the limits of genuine historical knowledge.

In addition, the interest in archaeological finds came to play a part in legislation and government statutes. In this respect Sweden gave the lead. There the decree of 1684 had had a decisive effect, but in 1734, after some years of work and discussion by a commission, the Riksdag (Parliament) modified it in certain important respects. It was now drafted so as to specify a two-thirds share for the Crown and one-third for the finder in the case of general finds where no owner came forward, but in the case of 'buried treasure and other objects found beneath the ground, the landowner shall take one half and the finder the other, providing the true owner cannot be traced. Any old coins, gold, silver, copper, metal, or other works of art are to go to the king. The compensation payable by the Crown shall be to the full value of the field, with a supplement of one-eighth that amount. This payment goes to the finder.' This marks a departure from the earlier practice of allotting equal shares to the Crown and to the finder. The direction of the move, to give the landowner and the finder an equal share and to eliminate the Crown prerogative, points clearly to influence from Roman Law. At the same time, the entire find had first to be offered to the king, so that no things of antiquarian value should be lost.[26]

In Denmark the old law, according to which the Crown had title to treasure-trove, was still in force, and in 1683 it was incorporated unchanged into the Danish Law of Christian V, except that in 1671 members of the aristocracy had been granted the privilege of keeping finds made on their land. Gradually, however, the law fell into abeyance and when, in 1736, a Renaissance gold chain was found in Naestved (Zealand) it became apparent at the legal hearing that the authorities, including the judge, were quite ignorant of the treasure-trove law. The king was prompted to set up a commission to overhaul these statutes, and appointed two distinguished jurists, both with antiquarian interests, Thomas Bartholin, a presiding judge and son of the Royal Antiquary, and Andreas Højer, the chief legal adviser to the king. Højer had studied coin finds, the fortification of Danevirke in Schleswig, and the second gold horn from Gallehus (south Jutland) which when it was discovered in 1734 resulted in a general upsurge of interest in prehistory. The draft submitted by the commission and accepted by the king in a proclamation of 22 March 1737 runs as follows: 'Gold, silver, metal, and all other treasure discovered either buried or concealed in the ground, in forests, in fields, or in dwelling-places, or elsewhere, if unclaimed, is designated treasure-trove and belongs exclusively to the Crown.'[27] In the wording of the actual definition there is a clear resemblance to the Swedish clauses of 1684 and 1734 (the words 'metal' and 'buried treasure' recur), but elsewhere there is an obvious difference. In Denmark the Crown prerogative persists unchanged, though the application of the term 'treasure-trove' has been widened to include all metal objects, not only those of gold and silver. Base metal objects are hardly of a comparable pecuniary value: that there is no comment to this effect can only mean, presumably, that the jurists in their caution did not wish to go beyond the scope of the original law but brought objects of antiquarian value under the provisions of the law by designating them as 'metal'. Ancient bronze coins in a treasure might be quite as valuable as those made of precious metal, as anyone with a knowledge of the subject was aware.

The Danish law was less effective than the Swedish in one respect: there was no provision that the finder should be reimbursed. Compensation was commonly paid in practice (the finders of the gold horns, for example, both received a reward) but from many quarters came a demand for the inclusion of a clause to this effect in the wording of the law. This was furthered by the royal proclamation of 7 August 1752, which, taking the statute of 1737 as a basis, further extended the application of the term 'treasure-trove':

'Although everything which is found on Danish territory buried or concealed beneath the ground or in forests, fields, or dwelling-places, or elsewhere, whether gold, silver, metal, or other treasure, belongs, if unclaimed, exclusively to the Crown as treasure-trove, yet it has been conceded as an inducement to those of our subjects who make such a discovery that anyone finding ancient coins or other objects that by virtue of age or special character display some rarity shall, on duly sending the same to the Exchequer, receive full reimbursement of the value of the piece from royal funds.'

One cannot but admire this gargantuan sentence couched in well-conceived Chancellery language. The antiquarian evaluation is to be on an equal footing with the fiscal, and this intention is evidenced too by the version of the proclamation used by the Exchequer, where it is stated that treasure-trove covers 'old coins and other things which by virtue of their age and other characteristics are rare rather than valuable'.[28] That is to say, the archaeological significance of the find came to be regarded as no less important than its intrinsic value. We have already seen that the significance of coins, bracteates, some types of ornament, gold horns, rune-stones and the like was fully appreciated, in that they were clearly of ancient origin.

The attitude toward flint objects was not so consistent. In the *Kunstkammer*, for instance, they were exhibited with the Natural History specimens and not classed as archaeological objects. It would therefore have been unthinkable in the first half of the eighteenth century to treat them as treasure-trove, for their nature and antiquarian value was not then understood. It follows that the law of treasure-trove depended upon the state of archaeological research: the proclamation gives no precise specification but leaves the decision, naturally enough, to the experts. That this position later gave rise to uncertainties should not be allowed to discredit the excellent definition worked out by experienced civil servants in the mid-eighteenth century. They were chary, of course, about actually enforcing the law, and this tradition of leniency explains the establishment of a great many private archaeological collections – especially in the eighteenth century, when even archaeologists with a knowledge of the law of treasure-trove did not hesitate to keep rarities, including gold objects, for themselves. Their passion for collecting outweighed any wish to enrich the royal *Kunstkammer*, which itself possibly did not impress as being more than a cabinet of rarities. Scholars like Bircherod, whose writings on conservation have already been mentioned, and Erich Pontoppidan, a leading cleric and university administrator, had substantial collections; Bircherod justified them, indeed, as a token of patriotism. In 1701 he had sounded a warning that Scandinavia was about to lose the burial monuments of her prehistoric inhabitants once and for all.[29] Superstition no longer held the peasants in thrall and the barrows were being ploughed over. Many finds were being thrown away, others melted down. At the same time there were enough alert individuals amassing private collections by rewarding the peasants for finds, to prevent Bircherod himself from acquiring as much as he would have liked. He described the barrows and enumerated the

29 Erik Pontoppidan (1698–1764)

types of artifact produced from metal, for the most part a sort of yellow copper: daggers, knives, bracelets, rings, etc. But he also realized the importance of flint objects – daggers so skilfully fashioned that he doubted whether any contemporary of his would be able to work the hard flint so well, knives, arrows, axes, mallets, adzes, etc. – seeing in them weapons and tools. On the other hand, the great collector of folk-songs, Peder Syv, who had been present at the excavation of megalithic tombs containing flint objects in Zealand, still held to the opinion that they were thunder-stones; he also mentions the discovery of a large tooth in a grave near Birkerød as proof that giants existed in prehistoric times and as confirming the historicity of the folk-songs, in which giants frequently figure.[30] When several years later this tooth – by then on show in the *Kunstkammer* – was identified as that of a horse, its importance as evidence was nullified. It was only with the excavation of a 'jaettestue' or so-called 'giant's chamber' at Jaegerspris in 1744, conducted by Pontoppidan and the crown prince (later Frederik V), that rational methods were introduced into antiquarian investigations.

These two gentlemen were in residence at the royal palace in north-west Zealand, Pontoppidan being then court chaplain. They discovered the tomb at the edge of a path in the park, and carried out a careful excavation, noting the structure of the tomb and the finds it contained. Pontoppidan reported on it in the first volume of the Proceedings of the Danish Royal Society, as already mentioned, and the crown prince saw to the erection of a memorial tablet inscribed with a résumé of this report in well-turned Latin – hardly of much help to inquisitive local people who slipped in to take a look! The report was originally printed in Danish.

On the east side of the barrow, a little below the surface, were discovered two urns containing cremated bones and small metal objects 'which the deceased had for ornament or other use'. On the south side the excavators encountered a stone-built passage, 3 feet in length and breadth, which led to a large stone chamber

10 feet long by 8 feet wide by 7 feet high, constructed with the smooth sides facing inwards. Carefully removing the soil, they uncovered three skeletons in this chamber and one in the passage. Also in the earth-fill here they turned up 'two sharp-edged flints of the sort peasants call thunder-stones, but which in fact formed the tip of an ancient spear or other weapon'. These sensible and reliable observations are typical of his judgment on the finds. The size of the skeletons led him to conclude that the interred were normal human beings and to dismiss the notion that giants were buried in megalithic graves of this sort. (As late as 1727, in a report on a find near Assens, this explanation was still advanced.) It puzzled Pontoppidan and the valet Bruun, who had a knowledge of anatomy, that one of the skulls had a markedly receding forehead.

The result of these investigations was to show that the so-called 'giant's chamber' was a human burial-site. It was necessarily older than the urns (four in all) found lying above it, which belonged, naturally, to the cremation period, introduced with the coming of Odin, the high god of the Æsir (according to Icelandic tradition). Previous to this the Celtic or Cimbrian inhabitants had inhumed their dead: Pontoppidan, therefore, guessed that the tomb might be even older, but did not venture to adopt such an early dating. His ideas are summed up judiciously on the inscribed tablet above the tomb: 'This tomb, built by our pious, though heathen, forefathers at least 1800 years ago to contain the earthly remains of four deceased, and roofed with gigantic stones, was respectfully uncovered in June 1744 and furnished with this memorial tablet by His Highness Prince Frederik, heir to his forefathers' realms and noble qualities, the hope, the glory, and the joy of his people.'

In 1763 Pontoppidan summarized the results of his antiquarian studies in the introduction to his great work on Denmark.[31] It was natural for him to outline here the country's early history, and as illustrations he selected pictures of prehistoric ethnic types and monuments, partly taken from other writers, and drawings of exhibits in various archaeological collections, including his own. He gives a fresh interpretation of the finds, arguing on much the same lines as his older contemporary in Lund, Kilian Stobaeus, and combines it with theories based on literary evidence, as was customary at that time.

On the other hand, he tries to steer clear of the wildest fantasies, such as the migration of the prehistoric population from Babylon to the North, and bases his reconstruction on the actual finds, just as he had done in the report on Jaegerspris, and also on the testimony of rune-stones, Classical writers and the Old Norse tradition. He handles this literary evidence with particular ingenuity, basing his chronology on the arrival of Odin and his tribe from the Caspian Sea around 100 BC, they having introduced a knowledge of metals from the south-east at the same time as the Cimbrians, who had returned to their homeland from the south, and having cremated their dead.

Pontoppidan's hypothesis was that the previous culture had been a Stone Age one, characterized by inhumation and the use of weapons and tools, 'clubs, war-hammers, adzes, and knives of

30 A warrior of the Cimbri tribe, as illustrated by Pontoppidan in his *Danske Atlas* on the basis of an earlier model. (M. T. Arnkiel, *Cimbrische Heyden-Religion*, 1702)

polished flint'. These were so sharpened as to facilitate striking and cutting. The notion of thunder-stones he rejected out of hand.

In the later Metal Age, the migrations of the Angles, Saxons, Goths and Normans took place, and that provided a good basis for an account of more recent prehistory.

He described the burial-sites, aptly, as 'a veritable archive of information on Scandinavian history'. Generally the finds were of stone or base metals and thus valueless except in the hands of an informed researcher, who 'could make reasonable guesses from them as to the way of life of our forefathers and the resources at their disposal, and could judge from the quality of the crafts-manship what level the Ancients had reached in art and science'.

As a trained theologian he could scarcely refrain from com-menting on the grave-goods: 'They buried the dead man's weapons, ornaments, and other belongings with the corpse in the belief that he would need them in the other world and would find them there, not in their present shape but in a quintessential form; for they believed steadfastly in the immortality of the soul and in an after-life.'

All in all Pontoppidan worked from the finds themselves in his account of the prehistoric period, and attempted to use only the most trustworthy sources.

A later scholar and theologian Frederik Münter, who was both a professor and, later, bishop of Zealand, worked under more propitious circumstances. Before we consider this man's contri-bution, which led to important advances in the nineteenth century, we should take note of a revival in the vogue for pre-history in the other Scandinavian countries. Ideas in one country may have fruitful repercussions elsewhere in Scandinavia, as we have seen.

In the years after Hadorph's death the functions of the Swedish Royal Antiquary and the Antiquities Archive were much dimini-shed. An interesting excavation was carried out in 1724 (of a barrow in Uppland) but by and large little attempt was made to emulate the ambitious programmes of the seventeenth century. The Royal Antiquary in office between 1779 and 1786 allowed the collections, apart from those of coins, medals and archaeological material, to be dispersed among other institutions. The Vitter-hetsakademi was also in a state of atrophy, and though, through King Gustav III, it received new statutes on 20 March 1786 and a change of name, to Kungl. Vitterhets-, historie- och anti-kvitetsakademi (i.e. Royal Academy of Literature, History and Antiquities), this new infusion of purpose – typified by the appoint-ment of the Royal Antiquary as Secretary – proved unavailing with all but a few talented and enthusiastic individuals.

It was elsewhere, in the Universities of Lund and Åbo, that real advances were made, through the labours of gifted scholars with a dedicated interest in prehistoric remains. It can scarcely be accidental that precisely these two distinctive provinces, Skåne and Finland, should have fostered this type of research; for the newly arrived Swedish families soon developed a marked regional consciousness and were keen to learn about the special features of their province.

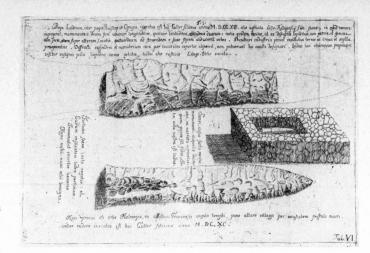

31 Two flint daggers, one from a stone cist in Scania, published by Kilian Stobaeus in *Ceraunii betulique lapides* (1738). The daggers are accurately drawn, as can be seen by comparison with the originals in the University Historical Museum, Lund

31

32 The Kivik burial-mound. This drawing by E. Feldt (1756) shows distinguished visitors at 'Breda Röhr', the name by which the grave is known locally. In the right-hand bottom corner of the drawing the artist has reproduced the pictures on the stone slabs of the inner chamber

Kilian Stobaeus, Professor of Natural Science at Lund, had correspondingly wide responsibilities. He kept a collection of naturalia and archaeological objects – and his classification of stone specimens is especially accurate. In an article of 1738[32] on the so-called thunder-stones he reviewed the various theories advanced since the Classical period and supplied illustrations of two flint daggers from his collection. One of them had been discovered in 1713 in a megalithic monument 20 feet long by 8 feet wide and 4 feet deep. While the drawing of the daggers is accurate – they can still be seen in the University museum – the sketch of the monument was executed from the description of the finder, who, one suspects, was guilty of some serious lapses of memory. Stobaeus was quite clear as to the nature of the flint daggers and other flint items: 'There can be no question that the oldest everyday implements, up to the time when the working and use of iron became known, were fashioned from flint.' He compared the objects with primitive tools used by hunting peoples – in Louisiana,

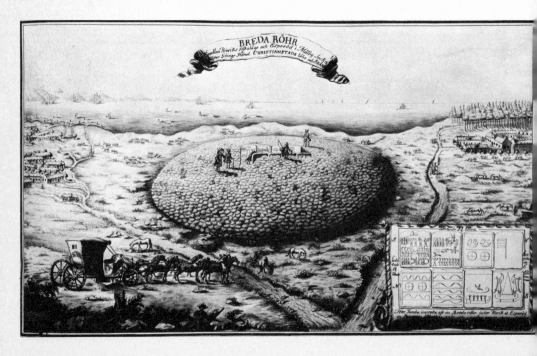

for instance – comprising sharp stones, animal teeth, etc., such as are to be seen, for example, in the royal *Kunstkammer* in Copenhagen. In his view the finds pointed clearly to a very old cultural stage, and he backed up his contentions by citing Lucretius and other Classical writers.

In 1735 Stobaeus presented his collection to the University of Lund, where it became the nucleus of the historical museum.

Shortly after his time the famous Bronze Age grave at Kivik in eastern Skåne was discovered. Although no antiquary took part in this strange excavation it may be worth mentioning, as typical of the fortunes of archaeology at that period.[33] On 14 June 1748 two small-holders set about removing stones from a large cairn to build stock-pens. As evening approached they happened on a long stone cist, with its promise of great treasures. They lit their pipes at sunset to ward off evil spirits and kept on feverishly digging. Rumours started to circulate in the fishing village: it was odd that the men did not return home. People flocked out to the scene, especially the boys, and eagerly joined in the search of the spacious burial-chamber. This little drama, punctuated with dull thumps from the barrow, lent atmosphere to the summer night.

The local government official after a while remembered the law of 1734: he called an inquiry, where the defendants averred that the extent of their finds was a broken metal button (picked up by a boy), a coin-like object (in which three boys had a share), an oblong piece of metal with a point (uncovered a fortnight later by the schoolmaster and the property-owner), and, finally, nails and the fragments of a circular metal vessel. Since the large vertical stones had been upturned, it is scarcely surprising that the authorities declined to accept these depositions and charged the two finders with concealing treasure; but after a long hearing at the regular autumn sitting of the court on 22 October, they were cleared of having withheld any Crown property and discharged.

It is peculiar that no one should have noticed the designs incised on the stone slabs, but in the years between 1750 and 1780 antiquaries visited the site frequently and copied these figures, the significance of which was much debated, some far-fetched theories being put forward.

Interest in the ancient monuments was coupled with a feeling of close kinship with the early ancestors. Here the Sagas helped to lend the distant past a heroic aura. When the brilliant sculptor J.J. Sergel was asked to make a sketch of a monument for the murdered King Gustavus III, he chose – among other subjects – a prehistoric tumulus with 'runic stones'.

In Denmark and Sweden antiquarian studies were among the

33 Sketch for a monument to King Gustavus III by the well-known artist Johan J. Sergel. Modelled on the prehistoric *ättehög* (tumulus), this design was executed (but not accepted) just after the assassination of the king in 1792

activities of the newly founded learned societies, and the same applies in Norway to the Norwegian Royal Society, centred on Trondheim.[34] Merely to mention the names of the founders is to vouch for this society's status – P. F. Suhm, an exceptionally well-read scholar, and G. Schøning. These men shared an interest in prehistoric research and enjoyed the support of Bishop Gunnerus. They set up an archaeological collection which was opened to the public in 1787 and formed the basis of the Videnskabsselskabets Museum. Excavations were soon got under way; the impulse behind them, typically enough, was Schøning's edition of Snorri's *Heimskringla*. In the introduction to this edition he had identified a very large barrow on the island of Lekkøe in Nummedal with the barrow which Snorri said King Herlaug had built for his brother and himself. King Harold Hardrada came on a raiding expedition, so the story went, and Herlaug and his twelve companions slipped inside the barrow, armed with provisions, and had themselves walled in. A local tradition on Lekkøe agreed quite well with this account. Meanwhile, wishing to test his theory, Schøning requested Lieutenant-General von Krogh to conduct the excavation. Man-power was readily available in the shape of infantry from the near-by training centre, and the first season began in 1778. Krogh was excited when he saw the results, and supplies of food and drink kept the soldiers 'willing, enthusiastic even, since Norwegians love their Fatherland and its antiquities'. Great quantities of animal bones and beams with rivets were found. In 1780 the landowner permitted Lieutenant Sommerschildt to do another season's digging, using estate labour. Skeletons from two interments came to light, leading Schøning (the authority for this account) to speculate that Snorri had been misinformed on the size of Herlaug's retinue. But the *Heimskringla* story seemed to be substantiated by the finds of woodwork, which were viewed as the structural component of a large burial-chamber.

After the death of his wealthy wife in Trondheim, Suhm moved to Copenhagen, and there used up a substantial part of the estate in enlarging his huge library and pursuing his historical studies, which were chiefly of the earliest period. He was charmed by the speculative reconstructions of prehistory so brilliantly advocated in Rudbeck's *Atlantica*. He paid proper regard to Dano-Norwegian tradition, while at the same time drawing on the achievements of Swedish scholarship. In his historical survey of the early Scandinavian peoples[35] he stated that the Danish royal line, which counted among its number such heroes as Skjold, Rolf Krage, Ragnar Lodbrog and (better documented) Gorm the Old and his descendants, could be traced back to Odin. He maintained that the ancient history of the Danes, with its vicissitudes, originated in the year 865 BC subsequent to the Tower of Babel, 1,758 years after the Creation, when a horde of peoples migrated northwards from Babylon toward Scandinavia, covering 420 miles every 101 years. The precise route could be indicated.

A later period of crucial importance was marked by the Cimbrian emigration from Jutland: first, Suhm pointed out, the island-dwellers attempted to take possession of the peninsular region; later, around 70 BC, there was an incursion of the Æsir, led by

Odin, from the lands bordering on the Caspian Sea. In this way Denmark regained the focal position in Scandinavian history which Rudbeck had denied her.

Suhm's theories became widely known and accepted in subsequent years. One popularization of them is found in the ballet *Sigrid*. He amplified his ideas in a school textbook, which came into common use; yet not long after the turn of the nineteenth century they began to look dated and were superseded by more realistic views. It is worth noting that Suhm postulates a sequence of stone, copper and finally iron weapons for the period between the coming of Odin and *c.* AD 800. How he reached this conclusion is obscure, but presumably he relied on Classical authorities like Lucretius, perhaps synthesizing their statements with the results of Pontoppidan's excavations.

The chief motive force behind antiquarian studies in Finland was the University at Åbo, and that may be ascribed in part to the presence there of the distinguished scholar Henrik G. Porthan.[36] In 1782 he published his *Plan till en Sockne-Beskrifning*, a work advocating a parish-by-parish description of Finland, in which he lists the ancient remains that ought to be recorded: prehistoric monuments, cult sites and ruins. Various pastors had already started work on such a description, partly at the prompting of the Royal Antiquary in Stockholm. Archaeological collections were formed – one such private collection was presented to the University of Åbo in 1770 – and excavations were carried out. In the van of these activities was Chr. Ganander, who in 1782 brought out his 'short account of burial mounds and cairns to be found in the parish of Lailela'. Other clerics wrote on prehistoric forts and Lapp settlements, and a number of publications ensured that the fruits of this widely based and thorough research were made available to the general public. Coin-finds were also dealt with: in 1755 the orientalist C. A. Clewberg produced a study of Arabic dirhems; others considered coins from the Roman and later periods. The result was the startling theory that the coins had been introduced in order to bribe the Finns into accepting Christianity. Altogether one senses a lively interest in prehistoric finds and a whole-hearted effort to understand them.

This appreciation manifests itself continually, in diverse ways. The work of Suhm influenced the great poet Johannes Ewald to write plays on Old Norse themes. Another equally interesting development was the laying-out of landscaped gardens to celebrate figures from the heroic past. In two parks, those at Ledreborg and Jaegerspris, a special attempt was made to instruct the public through a sort of permanent exhibition:[37] busts, statues and obelisks were erected in memory of the earliest kings and mythological figures. We owe this conception to two prominent men with antiquarian tastes, M. Hübner and H.P. Anchersen, who prevailed on the noble landowner at Ledreborg to illustrate Nordic mythology and prehistory in this tangible fashion. Anchersen had reason to single out Ledreborg as an ideal location; in 1745 he had designated the near-by Hertha Valley as the cult-centre of the goddess Nerthus, as described in Tacitus' *Germania*. They were somewhat optimistic in their approach: to represent

all these edifying great men of antiquity would require, they argued, a mere 381 monuments. Only a small group were actually completed in 1756–7, among them statues of Odin and Canute the Great and the obelisk for Harold Blue-tooth. The epigraph on this obelisk illustrates the educative principle behind the project: 'Harold Blue-tooth, son of Gorm: 28th king of Denmark: regnant AD 931–981: builds Jülin, or Jomsborg, on Wolin. Is christened by Poppo after the war against Emperor Otto I: establishes bishoprics in Slesvig, Ribe, Aarhus, and Odense.' This text is the counterpart of the explanatory labels in modern museums: it is characterized by pedagogic zeal, as becomes clear when compared to its nearest parallel – and possibly also its model – the Temple of British Worthies at Stowe Park, in England.

Ledreborg was a distinguished aristocrat's estate, its owner the head of the Danish Chancellery; his edifying open-air museum impressed the leading minister Høegh-Guldberg so much that he had a similar one set up beside the royal palace at Jaegerspris. The publication of Malling's book recording 'great and good deeds by Danes, Norwegians and Holsteiners' was conveniently timed to provide Høegh-Guldberg with the *raison d'être* for his project: all the noble people of Malling's title would be commemorated with stelae, and a special place of honour was to be reserved for the most senior personalities.

A site with just the attributes required became available when the three 'Vaeverhøje' were excavated in 1776. Like the previous excavation at Jaegerspris, the operations were supervised by a member of the royal house, Prince Frederik, heir presumptive to the throne and son of the Frederik whose work on prehistoric graves in the vicinity thirty-two years before has already been noted. Høegh-Guldberg now arranged for one of the tumuli to be fittingly converted, by incorporating the finest garden design, into an important part of the commemorative park.[38]

The excavators had entered the chamber of this megalithic tomb from the south side without observing any passage and they dug the entire central area. The chamber measured 24 feet in length and 4 to 6 feet in breadth and was 6 feet high at the centre. Digging down through this level they uncovered many human bones, including the skeleton of an adult whose height was estimated from the femur to be just on 6 feet; the skull showed the man to be fully grown. The following finds were recorded: the

corroded traces of a bronze weapon, a 'sacrificial knife' (presumably a blade or a dagger), four axes and war hammers, all of flint, with honed edges, a 'small flint fork, two inches long, with two prongs' (actually an arrowhead!), amber and an ornamented slate pendant. Outside the chamber in the mound they found urns containing bronze objects and cremated bones.

Since Høegh-Guldberg believed the stone objects to belong together, he accorded the tomb a very early dating; the two other mounds also contained bronze objects in association both with skeletons and urns. There was no trace of iron in any of these mounds, which supported his view that all three of them were very ancient.

When the investigation was complete the burial-chamber was opened to the public, but not before being embellished with a stylish entrance portal dedicated to Prince Frederik's mother, Queen Juliane Marie, after whom the mound was now named Julianehøj. The domed top of the mound was re-shaped to form terraces, which were linked to each other and to ground-level by several flights of steps. The planting of trees was meant to underline further its character as a piece of classical landscape design. A Norwegian rune-stone was set on a column at the highest point. The stone, which had been sent to the king, together with rich grave-goods, was to bear witness to the generations that had peopled Denmark-Norway in prehistoric times and speak to posterity through its runic epigraph.

The founders of the kingdom were honoured by a circle of stelae on the terrace immediately below. Here the contemporary royal house paid homage to its most distant predecessors – the Danish kings Dan and Harold War-tooth, the Norwegian Harold Hardrada, and Widukind, the head of the house of Oldenburg.

Deep down in the mound the visitor makes his respectful way into the dark stone chamber, which, lit only by the flickering of a hanging lamp, is now a room sacred to the memory of the earliest, nameless member of the people who had originally established the kingdom. Here a man of aesthetic sensibility and antiquarian tastes might pause, on an earthen bench preserved by the excavators for this purpose, and enjoy the glint of the lamp on the smooth sombre stone walls.

In the same year, 1776, the new, Romantic style of landscape design, which made use of prehistoric motifs, became fashionable. Renouncing the rectilinear emphases of baroque style, the Romantic garden sought to recapture the variety of Nature in winding paths, clumps of trees, unexpected views and evocative scenes. Bizarre elements like hermits' cells, with dead men's bones and other intimations of mortality inside, were sufficient to give most visitors a macabre thrill. But more relevant to our purpose is the faking of prehistoric monuments to achieve this kind of atmospheric effect in gardens.[39]

The 'tumulus' surrounded by a massive stone ring in the park at Moesgaard, south of Aarhus, is an early example. Standing by a hermit's shelter one gains a view, across a small woodland lake, of this formidable pile, which is crowned by a huge locust-tree and some sombre yews.[40] Truly a place that conjures up the distant

34 (*Opposite*)
Obelisk for King Harold Blue-tooth in the 'Real-Akademi' at Ledreborg, Zealand

35

35 (*Opposite*)
The Julianehøj (Jaegerspris, Zealand) was adapted, after excavation, to serve as a monument to the glorious past

36 A fake prehistoric tumulus
with a surrounding stone circle
at Moesgaard, Jutland

past, it calls to mind Chr. Pram's play *Staerkodder*, and enables
us to savour lines like

> O friendly grave, in your shade there is peace;
> your silent denizens feel no sorrow.

Barrows were also revered as the last resting-places of ancient
warrior heroes. Artists became aware of their pictorial value;
outstanding painters like Jens Juel and Abildgaard introduced
them into landscapes or treated them as symbols.

Nor need it surprise us that enterprising sculptors such as
Wiedewelt set themselves to study prehistoric relics in the countryside and in galleries, to get ideas for the garden novelties and designs
for plays and ballets with ancient settings which they were expected to turn out. Wiedewelt had also been in England, and his
study of landscape gardening in its original home no doubt gave
him further inspiration. In the palace garden of Fredensborg he
executed an 'enigmatic relic from Antiquity' – a fairly strange
dolmen with antique busts. The dolmen was reproduced in a
painting by Abildgaard – now known only from a sketch, as the
original picture was destroyed when Christiansborg in Copenhagen was burnt down in 1797.

37 The so-called 'enigmatic
relic', a fake *dysse* with antique
portrait busts, in the palace
garden at Fredensborg, Zealand

38 N.A. Abildgaard's 'Europe
in the primeval period', a sketch
for a painting at Christiansborg
(1794). The *dysse* is shown in the
upper part of the sketch

The presence of this motif in art and garden design should be seen as reflecting a growing general interest in prehistory. The young cosmopolitan scholar Frederik Münter, son of an immigrant German priest, was infected by this enthusiasm in Denmark, besides being influenced by his acquaintanceship with the poet Ewald. He tried to find out the true nature of the prehistoric monuments by studying them *in situ*.[41] While still a student, in 1780, he explored places like Lejre and reported on them in level-headed fashion; he also made a point of visiting the antiquarian gardens at Ledreborg. Later in the same year he carried out an excavation of King Sweyn's barrow, near Pederstrup on the island of Lolland, and was actively assisted by the property-owner, Count Reventlow. The stone-built chamber, 12·5 metres (40 feet) long, was examined and drawn, and the young archaeologist wrote a detailed description, one which – sad to say – was not enlivened by sensational finds. The sole discoveries were human bones and horses' teeth.

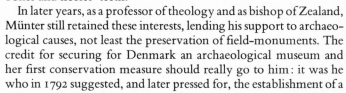

39 Frederik Münter (1761–1830)

In later years, as a professor of theology and as bishop of Zealand, Münter still retained these interests, lending his support to archaeological causes, not least the preservation of field-monuments. The credit for securing for Denmark an archaeological museum and her first conservation measure should really go to him: it was he who in 1792 suggested, and later pressed for, the establishment of a

'collection of all the Nordic monuments and prehistoric objects which are either extant or on which there exist accurate and reliable reports – a task whose urgency is enhanced by the destruction overtaking these monuments at the hands of peasants, and through public works as well; since many ancient burial-mounds, assembly places, and sacrificial sites have been destroyed by road construction in Zealand, and that even those examples renowned in tradition should not have been spared is universally acknowledged and deplored.'

The important effects of Münter's scheme will be described later. His proposals owe much to his method of presentation, yet their success must be attributed not only to the clarity of his reasoning but also to the newly won antiquarian interest of the leading circles in society stimulated by artists and scholars – an interest that was shared by much of the nation.

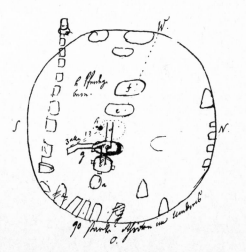

40 Münter's drawing of King Sweyn's tumulus, near Pederstrup, Lolland

Chapter Four

Classification and Protection of Archaeological Material in the First Half of the Nineteenth Century

IN Copenhagen, the administrative and intellectual centre of Denmark-Norway, there was mounting pressure for a stop to be put to the steadily increasing destruction of ancient monuments and for archaeological objects to be housed in a museum. Many supported the proposals of Münter, or came forward with schemes which closely resembled his. When his plan was eventually put into effect, the result, initially, was a commission, which with time evolved into two permanent institutions, each under a distinguished and gifted director. The first stages, however, were modest enough.[42]

The need for a public collection was perhaps not obvious, since one already existed in the shape of the *Kunstkammer*, or Royal Collection, at Christiansborg. The problem with this collection, however, was that it contained so much: the visitor had difficulty in deciding what prehistory really was. But exciting prehistoric exhibits were to be seen, such as the two massive gold horns from Gallehus, and a visitor with real perception, like Stobaeus, could compare objects in the Indian Room with the flint artifacts in the Cabinet of Naturalia. The admission charge was rather high: for a party of six or seven visitors it was two Danish dollars – not to mention six marks in gratuities.

One fanciful proposal put forward was for a monument park containing a 'ruin-mountain . . . with Valhalla'. This represented the Romantic garden in its most eccentric flowering, and it would be interesting to know exactly how the projected Valhalla was to have been realized.

A more realistic set of proposals was advanced by Professor Rasmus Nyerup, who was indebted for his ideas to A. Lenoir's Museum of French Monuments in Paris, set up by the new Republic in 1801. The rich collections assembled there consisted of numerous ancient remains confiscated during the Revolution. In 1806 Nyerup brought out a book outlining his ideas as to how material from prehistoric Denmark-Norway should be exhibited in the projected museum. This book, titled *Survey of the National Monuments of Antiquity, such as may be displayed in a future National Museum*, was actually the fourth volume of his descriptive account of prehistoric and latter-day remains. During the travels he undertook in order to prepare this work, Nyerup became aware of how negligently ancient monuments were being treated. He inveighed against this vandalism and after a discussion of previous antiquarian work he put forward the idea of a museum of prehistory, a rune-

41 R. Nyerup (1759–1829)

hall, and commemorative rooms for the Middle Ages, which were considered to close with the sixteenth century. A detailed survey of previous archaeological inquiry, it contains lively quotations, some drawn from contemporary Romantic poetry.

A period of setbacks on the national level, ushered in by the defeats of 1801 and 1807 at the hands of the English, had its effect in stimulating enthusiasm for the grandeurs of the ancient past: consolation could be sought in memories of Danish antiquity. In advertisements for the ballet *Ragnar Lodbrog* it was intimated that that stage weaponry would be 'genuine old Nordic Props'. Suhm's Sigrid story, which, with its author's penchant for precision, was set between AD 155 and 177, was also staged as a ballet. There was a vogue for prize essays and learned articles in the field of Scandinavian archaeology; highly ingenious theories were yet again put forward to explain thunder-stones and flint weapons.

But there was another, more immediate factor behind this change in the national consciousness. During the night of 4 May 1802 the Gallehus gold horns were stolen from the *Kunstkammer*.[43] 42 Despite police activity, it was not until 7 May that the public was informed of the theft. The culprit, moreover, was only discovered when he was indiscreet enough to begin selling large quantities of clasps, Indian coins and other fakes manufactured from the gold of the melted-down horns.

Not far from the foundry where this had been done was the boarding-house where the young Adam Oehlenschläger wrote his spirited poem on the loss of the horns. This work marked the inception of the Romantic movement in the North. It was a bitter and courageous denunciation, a crusade against apathy and against his country's decline from a glorious past.

About the theft there was nothing heroic. Custodial ineptitude played a large part. The thief struck up an acquaintance with the keeper and secretly borrowed a key. A duplicate was quickly produced. The other key to the *Kunstkammer* was identical with his own door-key.

On the evening of 4 May the thief let himself into the vestibule off the Palace Square and crept up the staircase to the first storey, where the door, normally locked, had been left open because of water damage. With the help of his two keys, he made his way through the gallery to the Hall of Heroes and into the Cabinet of Antiquities, having no need for a light. Smashing the glass of the display case, he removed the two heavy gold horns and returned home without attracting attention. The horns were melted down, and it is part of the tragedy of their loss that all the casts prepared

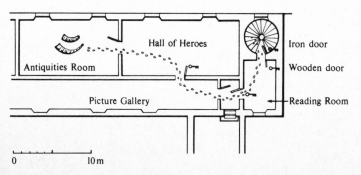

42 The theft of the gold horns: a sketch of the upper floor of the *Kunstkammer*, showing the route taken by the thief on the night of 4 May 1802 (after J. Brøndsted)

19

from them had disappeared. All we have now is some fairly reliable illustrations and brief descriptions. The loss is the more unfortunate in that these horns represented a unique source of information on Scandinavian cultural history.

Oehlenschläger was not alone in his veneration of Denmark's forefathers. When, in 1801, a memorial was proposed for those who had fallen in the naval engagements outside Copenhagen harbour, a commemorative tumulus with standing stones was erected. The tumulus was built in accordance with ancient Scandinavian practice and the stones were set up in a fashion designed 'to recall the prehistoric *bauta* stones' (memorial stones).[44] The monument

33

designed by the Swedish artist Sergel to commemorate the murdered King Gustav III (1792), but never built, provides an interesting parallel.

The public, now alive to prehistory, watched with some astonishment as new finds made their appearance. Some bronze *lurer* (a form of long curved horn or trumpet) and other noteworthy objects were reported in the newspapers, only to vanish again later. As a large wooden crucifix which had been sold cheaply by the Roskilde cathedral authorities was being dismantled, what was to roll out but a small rare gold cross! The *Kunstkammer* acquired it for just over sixty Danish dollars. Meanwhile, the wholesale destruction of field-monuments continued.

This was a highly unsatisfactory state of affairs. In 1806 Münter published a small book giving a critical review of the situation. He chose to discuss a site which was familiar to everyone, the seat of

43

the saga kings near Roskilde, known as Lejre. In an effort to ensure the protection of these venerable remains, he sent a copy of his book, titled *Leire in Zealand at the beginning of the nineteenth century*, to the Chancellery, with a plea that 'the ancient monuments should not be destroyed'. In the meantime, Nyerup had received the first contributions of archaeological material toward the future national museum. He felt encouraged to appeal to collectors in the field of Scandinavian archaeology to donate their finds to the Cabinet of National Antiquities. He also tried to find the rune-stones which had been sent to Worm, but discovered only a few that lay scattered around the churchyard of Holy Trinity.

In the following year, 1807, when the Chancellery asked Münter for advice on how to set up a commission which would take charge of prehistoric monuments, his reply was prompt. By 22 May the crown prince had signed the following Chancellery recommendations, which followed Münter's proposals exactly.

'I Prehistoric monuments which are situated on farmland and are too large and bulky to be shifted must be divided into two groups, those which merit preservation through Royal proclamation and others of lesser importance which the landowner or tenant might be authorized to use as he sees fit.

II Measures must be devised to prevent important medieval remains in churches and other public buildings from being destroyed.

III Some appropriate way must be found of informing the peasantry about the value of archaeological finds. Such finds are

43 A *dysse* at Lejre, as illustrated by Münter in his *Leire i Sielland* (1806)

constantly being unearthed by farm-workers but they are usually destroyed, simply through ignorance of their true nature.

IV A State museum must be planned (for now that Professor Nyerup has raised the question such an institution seems to have become the public wish) which, at a minimum of expense to the State, could house all the archaeological objects to be found in His Majesty's domains, insofar as they already form part of the Royal collections or in the course of time might be incorporated into them.

V It must be considered how this museum could then be run for the benefit of the general public.'

It is interesting that Münter should have made no reference to the laws then in force in Sweden, which in principle went much further, but instead consulted the interests of the owners of monuments, a policy which has influenced legislators up to the 1930s in Denmark. He further proposed that the members of the Commission should be: Overhofmarskal A. W. Hauch, Director-in-Chief of the *Kunstkammer* and a man of great influence, who had previously been consulted and had consented to act as chairman; Monrad, a senior civil servant, Captain Abrahamson, and Professors Münter, Thorlacius and Nyerup, all of whom had been actively engaged in work on antiquarian remains. Nyerup was chosen as Secretary.

The Commission settled down to its work, selecting corresponding members in countries which had come under Danish and Norwegian influence. A select number of antiquaries was later appointed to increase the initial representation.

And in this way the Commission proceeded unobtrusively with its duties. Some monuments were placed under protection and a periodical, *Antiqvariske Annaler*, with articles on the matters in hand, began to appear. However, Nyerup realized, as time passed, that he could not take care of the museum's new acquisitions, which lay at one end of the loft in Holy Trinity Church, then the property of the University library. Here they were stacked in a steadily mounting heap.

It was then that Münter, in consultation with the other learned members, came out in favour of an enthusiastic young man named Christian Jürgensen Thomsen. The son of a wealthy merchant, Thomsen seemed an excellent replacement as Secretary because he needed no salary and was deeply interested in antiquity; he had already made a name for himself as a keen numismatist with a talent for classification. Münter described him as an

'amateur with a great range of accomplishments. I know him well personally. He is fully at home with Roman and Scandinavian numismatics and has a quite exceptional knowledge of art. In addition, he has a command of several living languages, in particular German, French, and English, and can write, I know, in the first two. He is a diligent worker and also, as Professor Nyerup points out, a man of independent means. It is true that although he has learnt Latin he is not a university student. I must insist, however, that in my opinion, given the present state of archaeological science, that is a point of minor significance. It

44 C.J. Thomsen (1788–1865)

45 These were some of the archaeological finds used by Thomsen in establishing the Three Age system. We see them arranged according to this system, with stone objects to the left, bronze ones in the middle and iron ones to the right. He expressly mentions the iron objects, from cremation burials at Ørnekullerne, Bornholm, as evidence for an iron age

matters not at all *where* a man gets his knowledge from, the important thing is *whether* he has it.'[45]

This sensible and unbiased recommendation from the most famous scholar of the time secured Thomsen his post. Soon after, he was to be seen sitting over a ledger, as if in an efficiently run business office, numbering specimens and entering them carefully with descriptions in a catalogue. By so doing he gained a first-hand knowledge of this extensive body of material, some five hundred items. Among them were several very fine flint artifacts, which he kept examining so as to familiarize himself with them.

Gradually the collection was brought into working order; with his very first year of museum work, in 1816, Thomsen laid the foundations of the system which subsequent generations have gone on to develop.

Thomsen saw that in order to make these finds comprehensible, the primary task was to classify and exhibit them. The Commission for its part attempted to take over the first storey of the Church of St Nicholas, then half in ruins, but did not succeed. The collection was to remain in the loft above the choir of Holy Trinity Church.

The first question Thomsen asked himself was: what principles of classification would he use? Münter had been correct in his assessment: a scientific basis was still lacking, and would have to be worked out. Now familiar with the finds, Thomsen concentrated on the different materials of manufacture and made these the basis of his classification. In a letter of 16 July 1818 to the Swede J.H. Schröder, a Professor of History, he outlined the principles he had adopted.[46] He decided to take as a basis three historical phases, beginning with the heathen period. This period in turn he subdivided as follows:

'1 Stone tools and weapons, 2 Metal and copper weapons and other battle-equipment, such as the *lurer*, and 3 Iron artifacts of the heathen period (these being among the rarest and most remarkable finds). You know from experience, I am sure, that objects like these are normally corroded away by acids in the soil – but now we have important specimens from Bornholm which escaped corrosion because the barrows in which they were buried were made of sand. 4 Household tools and utensils, 5 Ornaments,

45

6 Objects which were presumably used in the heathen cult, or had some connection with it . . ., 7 Burial urns, 8 Miscellaneous objects from the heathen period, not represented by any of the foregoing categories.'

Although Thomsen does not emphasize it, the first three categories represent three different historical phases, whereas the remaining categories apply to the whole heathen period. He was not at this point ready to link them directly with each of the phases.

It is easy enough to see how he arrived at this scheme. He examined the specimens themselves, noted which objects occurred as part of the same find, and compared his observations with previous ideas on the prehistoric period, available to him for example in Nyerup's *Survey of the National Monuments*. In this book were collected all previous observations of any consequence, including those of Pontoppidan. But the work of these predecessors provided merely an initial guide for Thomsen's own observations. He postulated an Iron Age from new finds made at cremation graves at the Ørnekuller, near Hasle on Bornholm, which he interpreted quite accurately; likewise, it is typical of him that, whereas he placed the earlier bronze objects in a Bronze Age, he did not take bronze objects of the Iron Age as a criterion where the Bronze Age is concerned, partly because of his knowledge of the combination finds, partly because he had a sharp eye for form and ornamentation and took features like these into account. A little later, in 1819, a young archaeologist from Lund, Sven Hylander, noted while on a visit to the 'Trinity' museum that Thomsen had arranged his exhibits in the following groups: 1 adzes, 2 axes, 3 hammers, 4 knives and 5 chisels, in other words a classification with respect to function and form.

Though at the time quite unheralded, a new science had come into being, a science whose principles were observation and classification. It relied on excavation and chance discovery for its resources, not on literary theories or Classical tradition. Of this Thomsen was perfectly aware, although he maintained an attitude of respect toward the members of the Commission. He wrote confidentially to a Swedish friend:

'For those who have derived their knowledge and their entire learning from books *alone* I have no sympathy. I have seen only too often what *utterly absurd* errors they fall into when they must turn their wisdom to practical use. So, my good friend, let us by all means buy books and read them attentively, but never neglect to look with our own eyes.'

Here we have the key to the new science: its prime requirement, if results were to be obtained, was a sharp-eyed observer.

For a time, the arrangement of exhibits at the museum had to suffice as a public exposition of Thomsen's ideas. Though a lively conversationalist and correspondent, he was curiously inhibited in writing for publication, and at times lamented his lack of facility as a stylist. It was not until many years later that he managed to issue a handbook on Scandinavian prehistory. But in spite of criticism he held firmly to his idea of three periods. This is how he expressed it in 1825 to a German scholar:

'I find it essential, in placing archaeological specimens accurately in context, to keep a chronological sequence in mind, and I believe that the validity of the old notion of first stone, then copper, and finally iron is constantly gaining new support in Scandinavia.'

To win acceptance for the theory it would be necessary to set up a large museum of finds, preferably group-finds like the one of 1817 from Tjurkö, which consisted of a gold bracteate and a solidus from the reign of Theodosius II.

Thomsen was at his most accessible with young people. Generous toward gifted artists and future archaeologists, he formed a particularly close friendship with two young Swedish scholars, Hylander, who died prematurely, and Bror Emil Hildebrand, whom he encouraged in times of adversity and advised in times of prosperity. With these men, whom he had initiated into numismatics and archaeology, he maintained a warm and unconstrained friendship throughout their lives. It is interesting that he could do this at a time – the first decades of the nineteenth century – when Sweden and Denmark were experiencing political crises. It was through Thomsen's visit to Lund in 1817 that Hylander and he first met, and subsequently there was a lively exchange of letters across the Øresund. Hylander accompanied Thomsen on an antiquarian study-tour of Skåne and later, in 1820, on an official round of inspection on Bornholm, where the Antiquities Commission had begun excavations.

During this period the Antiquities Commission carried out several seasons of digging.[47] Their investigation on Bornholm was the idea of two surveyors, Jansen and Lund, who were interested in studying prehistoric burials. Jansen suggested the use of soldiers to provide a labour force and Thomsen, remembering the important evidence that had previously come his way from Bornholm, threw his weight behind the proposal. Naturally the military commandant had to seek royal permission, and although Frederik VI was not himself interested in archaeology he granted it, on condition that only soldiers who volunteered were employed. Practically all of them settled for excavating rather than drill. Münter too was well-disposed toward the idea; during an official visit to Bornholm he had noticed prehistoric monuments and rocking-stones, taking them to be a kind of prehistoric oracle.

Jansen took charge of the excavations, for which the militia on Bornholm supplied a labour force of six hundred men, each man in turn doing a day's work. Worthwhile results were obtained. A number of burial-mounds were investigated, and Jansen demonstrated that such mounds might offer a sort of stratigraphy, that is to say, early and late burials. This is documented with a careful profile drawing.

All in all, the excavation plans and finds of prehistoric objects worked out well. Among their discoveries was a Bronze Age burial containing a sword and a palstave in a massive stone cist near Ypnasted; important finds from the transition between the Bronze Age and Iron Age were made in the Mandhøj in Ibsker.

Both Jansen and Lund found long dolmens of an early type on the island, as their drawings show, but unfortunately these have since been obliterated. Near Baekkegaard Lund investigated an interesting Bronze Age barrow containing several burials, and by the coast a settlement with (neolithic) potsherds. He drew and measured prehistoric remains which have since vanished, such as field systems, though with his limited archaeological background he did not recognize them for what they were.

A few years later, in 1824, Crown Prince Christian Frederik (son of the Frederik who had investigated the Julianehøj) renewed these excavations on Bornholm. In a mound north of Rønne he found a burial containing a skeleton and a bronze dagger. He dug two crosswise trenches on Gamleborg, a war-time hill-fort, and found potsherds which recent excavation near by has shown to date from the Viking Age. All this work was later described in a report.[48]

The new finds fitted naturally into the pattern which Thomsen had pointed out, and so did the 1820 excavation of the northernmost mound at Jelling. This was occasioned by the running dry of a cistern, normally full of water, at the top of the mound. The farmers proceeded to sink the well deeper and dug their way into a large timber-built room, a burial-chamber which had been plundered centuries before by robbers who had broken in through the roof. A few objects, lying inside and outside the burial, had been left behind – a small silver goblet, ornaments, and pieces of carved and painted wood. Such were the meagre prizes yielded up by this famous grave-site, allegedly the burial-place of King Gorm and Queen Thyra. The cistern, it now appeared, was actually the hole dug by the thieves in order to break in.

Apart from this, there were few properly conducted excavations at this time. One interesting example is the investigation of the remarkable Bronze Age burial near Hvidegaard, north of Copenhagen, in which several experts took part – the archaeologists Thomsen, Herbst and Strunk, together with a doctor named Ibsen, who prepared the organic remains and carried out anatomical studies.[49] Exceptional care was taken in uncovering this burial, with its textiles and leather pouch. The pouch yielded a whole assortment of bizarre objects, which Steenstrup, the zoologist, identified as a snake's tail, conches, the mandible of a rodent, etc. An ox- or calf-skin lay spread out beneath the buried

46 The Hvidegaard burial (near Kongens Lyngby, Zealand). This stone cist, which contained cremated bones and a fine array of male apparel, was excavated in 1845 by C.J. Thomsen and the anatomist Ib Ibsen, with the assistance of Strunk, Herbst, and, as a novice, the young artist Magnus Petersen. Among their finds was an oblong heap of burnt clothes, resting on a hide and covered by brown woollen clothing

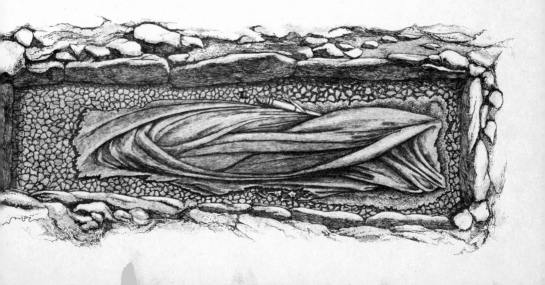

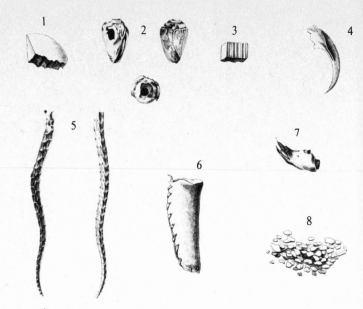

47 Contents of a leather pouch recovered from the Hvidegaard burial and no doubt thought to possess magical properties.
1, Fragment of amber bead; 2, three views of perforated conch (*Coneus mediterraneus Hwass*); 3, die of coniferous tree; 4, claw of bird of prey; 5, part of grass snake's tail, seen from two sides; 6, little leather bag; 7, part of lower jaw of young squirrel; 8, sample of small pebbles found in the leather bag. Not to scale

48 Christiansborg as it appeared in C.J. Thomsen's lifetime, viewed from the riding ground. To the left on the ground floor, the archaeological collection, exhibition and work rooms

49 Thomsen showing visitors round the Museum of Northern Antiquities, as he did regularly between eleven and one o'clock every Thursday from 1819 onwards. The lively interest this aroused was enhanced by such personal touches as placing the gold torc round a little girl's neck

objects. The grave-goods proper included a sheathed sword, a fibula, a razor, a knife and a pair of pliers.

Thomsen devoted his life to the museum; after the death of his father his entire time was spent there. He realized to the full two of Münter's objectives – to found a national museum and ensure its usefulness. Soon the museum became a public attraction. Thomsen was able to announce, as early as 1819, that it would be open once a week between eleven and one o'clock and, jovial and animated, he showed the visitors around in person. 48

The church-loft was not fit for a permanent exhibition and was, moreover, wanted by the library. In 1832 the Commission succeeded in acquiring five rooms in a wing of the palace of Christiansborg. Helped by the sympathetic King Christian VIII they got more and more rooms, until at last they numbered eighteen. However, as there were other demands on Christiansborg, the Prince's Palace opposite was in turn taken over by the Antiquities Museum in 1853. This had already in 1844 incorporated the royal *Kunstkammer*, supplementing its collections with a substantial number of pieces recovered under the law of Danefae.

Under Thomsen's tireless direction contributions were unpacked from their crates and sorted and the collection expanded into a well-ordered museum, containing more than twenty-seven thousand numbered items. Grants were exiguous, and he had few assistants, who at first were obliged to work voluntarily. Thomsen had an especially high opinion of Herbst, a diligent numismatist who followed the instructions of his Director respectfully. On the other hand, he was a little troubled by the young J.J.A. Worsaae, who was of an independent mind, and who combined a critical attitude with natural facility as a writer. Worsaae was obviously gifted but he differed in temperament from Thomsen, being enterprising and dynamic where the older man was cautious; he openly criticized what he did not hold with. Here lay the reason for the brevity of Worsaae's stay at the museum. None the less, defeatism was foreign to Thomsen's nature. He wrote in 1863: 'I know the customary excuses very well – no money, no space, no staff – but I also know how much can be done if one proceeds sensibly and patiently. When the people see concrete results, that things are being done and not just written about, there is immediately greater willingness to support us in our endeavours.' Another saying of his is worth recording: 'There is a standard which I often apply to museum directors, and indeed to much else as well; I ask, what did the man find when he took up his post and what did he leave behind him when he retired?'

Thomsen was responsible for the unassuming and down-to-earth manner in which the Royal Museum for Nordic Antiquities received its visitors. He understood how to touch his audience, as when he laid a heavy golden torc round a little girl's neck. By such means prehistory at once came alive for them. 49

His archaeological research was fundamental both in distinguishing the three periods and in the classification of artifacts. His contribution to a *Guide Book to Nordic Antiquity* (*Ledetraad til Nordisk Oldkyndighed*), published in 1836, treated antiquities in a solid and well thought-out manner. Here he brought his argu-

ments together, considering the three periods particularly in their relation to cultural history.

The earliest period, the Stone Age, was characterized by tools and weapons of stone, wood, bone, etc. The use to which these were put is indicated by the marks of wear they bear. Cultural evolution differed from one country to another, but the early inhabitants in Scandinavia had this much in common, that they resembled savages and apparently dressed in animal hides.

In the Bronze Age, ornaments, weapons and cutting tools were of bronze or copper; the explanation for the initial use of these metals, rather than iron, was clearly that copper was available in a pure and usable state in nature. To extract iron, on the other hand, entailed a complicated procedure, which could only have been learnt through sustained contact with southern peoples. This seems to have occurred earlier than the Roman imperial period, since by then the use of iron was already wide-spread in Scandinavia.

To this period belong both large stone cists and urns and also small stone cists, the latter containing cremated bones and small objects. Typical of Bronze Age decoration are concentric circles, running spirals, double spirals and wave patterns.

In the latest period, the Iron Age, iron was predominantly used, but bronze was never completely supplanted and objects of glass and silver also occur. Norway and Sweden were apparently the major areas of iron extraction. Both cremation and inhumation were practised and sometimes the dead man's horse was also interred. In artifacts of this period serpents and dragons appear as ornamental motifs (here Thomsen was thinking of Late Iron Age zoomorphic ornamentation).

The three periods are each characterized by certain features, primarily the materials of manufacture but also burial customs and

50 Types of Bronze Age artifacts, from C. J. Thomsen's *Ledetraad*. (a) Tweezers; (b) celts; (c) palstave; (d) 'tutulus'

51 In *Ledetraad* Thomsen showed that ornamentation, as well as form and material, could be used in dating artifacts. The top four of the types illustrated – wave, ring, spiral and double-spiral ornamentation – were common in the Bronze Age, whereas the bottom two – snake and dragon figures – belong to the Iron Age. Runes appeared solely with this later, never with the earlier type of ornamentation

decorative forms. Though Thomsen made these features elements in his chronological scheme, he also recognized their significance for cultural history. He formed a model – to use a modern term – chiefly on the basis of three main features.

His detailed classification both of artifacts and field-monuments was the fruit of years of observation, isolating features which appeared to be characteristic. This procedure can best be evaluated in connection with a group which especially interested him, the bracteates.[50] He began to study them in 1820, returning to the subject time after time in later years, but only in 1855 did he bring out his treatise. This was accompanied by a volume of plates, containing painstaking life-size illustrations of the objects. First he divided genuine bracteates into two groups: A, those which he considered as foreign, and B, Scandinavian examples. Group A was further split up into:

I 'Older Imperial Byzantine bracteates and coins used as gold bracteates, together with imitations of the coins of these emperors.'

Montelius and other scholars after him, using Thomsen as a basis, have kept the term 'A' for the imitations in Class I.

II Later bracteates.

Group B divides into six classes. III to VI are later types, whilst VII comprises 'guldgubber' (thin gold plates embossed with the figure of a man).

VIII 'Bracteates with more elaborate designs and, sometimes, standing figures.' This class has been called 'B' by Montelius.

IX to XI are all bracteates in which a head is depicted above a horse. Montelius takes them together as Group C but Thomsen's classification is more discriminating: IX has a 'head above a horse or other quadruped, with one or possibly two birds in front of the head.' X has a swastika sign in front of a head, which is normally shown above a quadruped. XI is more general – a head above a quadruped.

XII, corresponding to F in Montelius, has animal figures.

XIII has 'figures of dragons and snakes' (zoomorphic decoration) and corresponds to Group E in Montelius.

It is worth noting how Thomsen's classification has determined later research, as in the special studies of Montelius. Thomsen's strength lay precisely in his ability to point out characteristic features and to compare these features with others, so combining them in a classificatory and chronological system. He drew on other workers' excavations, studied group finds and stratigraphy, but above all else he was the master *par excellence* of scientific observation, indeed the founder of modern archaeology. Within Danish scholarship he was naturally the dominating personality, but his close friendships with other Scandinavian archaeologists, whom he encouraged and generously supported, made him a central figure in archaeology throughout the North.

C. C. Rafn, a contemporary of Thomsen's, possessed precisely that eagerness to publish results and material which Thomsen lacked. In 1825 he decided to found the Kongelige nordiske Oldskrift-Selskab (Royal Society of Northern Antiquaries). Although his main aim was to bring out editions of Old Icelandic

52 Bracteate types, as illustrated by Thomsen, A, imitation of the portraits on gold coins. B VIII, standing male figures; B IX, horse with human head. B XIII, zoomorphic interlace. Cf. Montelius, types A, B, C and D

texts, he also hoped to publish archaeological finds. He was in many ways Thomsen's opposite, a devotee of the literary anti-quarianism which Thomsen had rejected and a prey to various fanciful ideas. Meanwhile he pursued his scheme with industry, arousing unprecedented interest in the society, which could soon boast ample finances and a distinguished and cosmopolitan membership. In addition to the series of texts and other publica-tions, the society produced an annual review, which appeared regularly and was for several generations of archaeologists not merely a valuable publication but in fact the only one in the field.

In the first half of the nineteenth century Denmark came strongly under the influence of the Romantic movement, which had a special interest in prehistory. That long obscure era offered scope for fantasy, but it could also be used to set the whole history in perspective. In the sagas the Romantics found an important source.

The Romantic movement covered a wide field, finding impor-tant expression in painting. Through the work of painters the picturesque value of ancient monuments came to be appreciated. But here too the influence of Thomsen is a factor not to be neglected.

Among the poetic works which produced most impact may be mentioned Oehlenschläger's *The Golden Horns* (*Guldhornene*) and *The Midsummer Eve's Play* (*Sct Hans Aftens Spil*). Here we have the quintessence of Romantic thought. In the second poem, Oehlen-schläger sets his scene at a prehistoric tumulus in the Deer Garden and has Harlequin, who stands for pure common sense and selfishness, leap up on to this tumulus, stumble and cry out irritably:

> May the Devil take these barrows!
> They are not of the slightest use.
The Aesthete replies quietly:
> Beneath thy vault,
> low mound,
> daylight and noise are excluded.
> From ancient times thine urn stands,
> filled with ashes.
> Immovably it stands until the great clock strikes.

For the Romantic, such monuments had a special attraction; they were the favourite destination of his walking excursions.

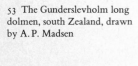

53 The Gunderslevholm long dolmen, south Zealand, drawn by A. P. Madsen

They loom up admonishingly in the moonlight: the ruined barrow and its rune-stone become a tragic symbol of the slighting treatment a corrupt modernity metes out to the past.

As the moon casts its light over the runes the Romantic continues in his state of reverie. The moon shone, just as it does now, on the man buried in the barrow. All sense of the time-span between that past and this present generation evaporates in this half-light; and the Romantic's thoughts drift back to the Age of Glory which once held sway, when heaven was upon earth.

> All is cold, sensible, empty!
> Filled with memories of great antiquity,
> I wander as among the dead.

Now antiquity becomes reality and the present a mere shadow-play. The present must be redeemed through the spirit of the past.

Ideas like these captured people's imagination. They went on walking tours to study prehistoric monuments and were stirred by the sense of mystery that surrounded them. Chr. Molbech and N.F.S. Grundtvig felt strangely moved by a visit in 1808 to the Gunderslevholm long dolmen in central Zealand, beautifully situated near a lake and surrounded by woods. They were entranced, as one would expect of the true aesthete. Each contributed an account of his experience to a journal that same year.[51] Molbech recounts the walk, their hesitant steps into the gloom of the forest, the sombre blackness. Making their way forward, they discover 'that splendid monument, perhaps far more than a thousand years old, in its surrounding of trees.' Molbech describes it in detail and concludes by explaining it as a sacrificial temple. They both contemplate, filled with 'reverence and solemn feelings, a memorial from the distant heroic age of Scandinavia – so complete, so characteristic, and now so rare – which prompts a more profound and much more vivid conception of the spirit of our forefathers than the finest treatise could do.'

Grundtvig gives his own impressions in the next issue of the periodical, concluding with these lines; strange enough for a young theologian:

> What rises yonder?
> O! is it not the altar's mossy stones,
> which the oak boughs thickly canopy?
> It is. O! I shudder,
> I tremble with pleasure,
> and my breast is filled with sacred reverence.
> I hasten, I hasten with winged feet
> to cast myself before the altar of Æsir,
> and praise the departed gods.

The ecstasy which the twenty-six-year-old poet experienced in his encounter with antiquity is fully matched by the sensible and convincing arguments which he advanced the following year, in the same periodical (7 October 1809), for the conservation of Danish prehistoric monuments. Unlike the Antiquities Commis-

53

sion, which wanted to preserve only a select portion of the monuments, Grundtvig adopted an uncompromising stand, contending that posterity must not be permitted to reproach his generation with having suffered their forefathers' graves to be destroyed:

'The special value which these monuments have for us is that, like embalmed heroes, they afford us a glimpse into the past and tell their own eloquent story about the lives and mighty feats of our forefathers. I consider barrows and stone circles which the farmers have so far spared to be without exception the property of King and Country; for no one pays taxes on them.'

The logical conclusion was that there should be a protection law corresponding to the law of Danefae, which Grundtvig clearly had in mind. How far he knew the Swedish laws is uncertain, but in any case a similarity is evident.

Meanwhile, the Antiquities Commission had set its members the task of selecting monuments, and recommended to the Ministry of Finance that three hundred should be protected. Their recommendations were accepted, but the Ministry took no steps to make conservation legally binding on the owners, and it was later discovered that several of the listed monuments had been removed. On the other hand, the protection order meant that numerous monuments were accorded special attention and so, in company with many more which had not been listed, escaped mishandling. The Commission distributed educational material, stressing that it seldom paid to dig for gold in burial-mounds.

The deep interest felt by the poets and later expressed in their works was also captured in the paintings of contemporary landscape artists.[52] Juel and Abildgaard had already noticed how ancient monuments lent character to their surroundings, but it was only with the next generation that prehistoric remains appeared as a favourite element in landscape paintings. The young artist 54 Johan Thomas Lundbye made particularly fine and sensitive use of this motif. He sought out such features deliberately, and if there were no tumulus or dolmen to be seen, he regretted their absence. The animals which lay beside the massive grey boulders or beside

54 The dolmen at Grønnaessegård, near Frederiksvaerk, drawn by J. Th. Lundbye

a mound entered into an intimate harmony with the monuments. It is not too far-fetched to suppose that Thomsen, the mentor of his youthful years, impressed upon the artist the significance of these remains. A lover of the open air, he was constantly making excursions into the Zealand countryside. 'But I must see a dolmen or a green barrow poking up out of a rye-field,' Lundbye wrote in a letter.

The Romantic movement, emerging nationalism and the bitter experience of defeat deeply affected the Denmark of Thomsen's generation, but similar currents of thought were evident in contemporary Sweden, Norway and Finland. In Sweden, the loss of Finland was an important factor. Between 1811 and 1845 a group of young poets and intellectuals came together, influenced by the Romantic conception of ancient ideals. It was in their lifetime that the national revival came about. From the name of their society, the Gothic League, and its statutes, it is apparent that their aim was to revive the ancient Gothic ideals of courage, integrity and a spirit of freedom. The periodical *Iduna* was founded, and it published quite a number of articles on early antiquity by antiquarian members such as Schröder, Tamm and Magnus Bruzelius. Poets like Tegnér and Geijer were widely read and admired, partly because of their Old Nordic themes.

At this period the Royal Antiquary had to protect both literary and material remains, and naturally his interests occasionally led him to favour one aspect of his work to the exclusion of the other. The current occupier of the post, Liljegren, tried valiantly to keep pace, but the heavy demands placed upon him proved too much. One of his projects, for example, was a collected edition of Swedish historical documents. So, in 1833, he took on an amanuensis to handle archaeological remains. The new appointee was Bror Emil Hildebrand, who had been suggested and discreetly recommended 55 by Thomsen. Thomsen had taken an interest in the promising young scholar, and was conversant enough with Swedish archaeology to know that it needed an infusion of talent.

Bror Emil Hildebrand had studied in Lund and continued work begun by Thomsen's friend Hylander, who had died young, on the Anglo-Saxon coins in the University museum. While engaged in this research, he came across some letters of advice from Thomsen, and when the monograph was printed Hildebrand included Thomsen's name in his list of acknowledgments. No more in the way of an introduction was needed: when, shortly after, Hildebrand came to Copenhagen, Thomsen awaited him expectantly. Though they met on comparatively few occasions, they became assiduous and intimate correspondents, each writing as frequently as three times a month. Hildebrand's period of study in Copenhagen lasted from 22 June until 17 August 1830. The crossing from Hälsingborg to Elsinore had taken three hours; the stage-coach left Elsinore for Copenhagen early the next morning and did not arrive until five o'clock in the evening. Every morning at six Hildebrand would make his appearance at Thomsen's house to study his coin collection, after which they would talk most of the morning; then Thomsen would leave for the Exchange, while Hildebrand stayed to read books which Thomsen owned or had

55 Bror Emil Hildebrand (1806–84)

on loan. They spent several days, of course, carefully examining the archaeological collection in Holy Trinity Church, and also visited other museums together.

In spite of the difference in their circumstances – Thomsen a recognized authority, forty-two years old, Hildebrand twenty-four and fatherless from an early age – an intimate friendship grew up between them which was greatly to affect Hildebrand's life. At times of uncertainty, as when Hildebrand's family were urging him to find a secure job, Thomsen helped him with sensible and authoritative advice. With almost fatherly solicitude, Thomsen saw that he stayed in archaeological research. For a time Hildebrand continued at Lund University, part of his work being at the museum. In the first few months after his return from Denmark he arranged the collection in accordance with Thomsen's scheme and opened it to the public for two hours a week. He was helped in preparing the exhibition by the detailed notes he had made on Thomsen's entire classificatory system. Thomsen felt, however, that Hildebrand ought to go to Stockholm and there build up a museum like the one which he himself, in spite of all obstacles, had successfully established. When Liljegren died a few years later, in 1837, it was Hildebrand who succeeded him, to Thomsen's whole-hearted satisfaction. In a long letter the older man showered him with sensible and cheerful advice, pointing out the following requirements:

1 To introduce system and order in the collection,
2 To ensure public access; the collection should not be exclusively for scholars,
3 To further archaeological science,
4 To engage one or two promising young men as assistants and eventual successors. Here he expressed regret at his own failure to find a suitable successor.

In a revealing conclusion he encouraged the young man to ward off feelings of despondency:

'After all, what sort of a future did I have, a merchant, trained for a commercial career and with no thoughts of any other possibility. Furthermore, when I began to sense the fascination of Art and Scholarship it was only by chance, without realizing it, that I came to the sources, which for me were the enticing thing. This was the opposite of a normal route, because I started from the objects themselves and from there came to the literature. And so the collections mattered to me more than the books. Did I not tell you what huge obstacles I had to contend with simply to see these collections – objects which later came into my keeping or which in various ways I wound up with the task of classifying, identifying, describing, etc., etc. I must see for myself, not through other men's eyes, though with me that's a longer process than it is with Hildebrand.'

He urged Hildebrand to be cautious, to think of his work first and himself second, and to get to know his assistants thoroughly before giving them appointments, if need be to pay them out of his own pocket at first rather than commit himself to them permanently;

it would not do to rely exclusively on one person, who might move somewhere else or turn out to be a failure.

With these benevolent words in mind, Hildebrand set about his work. Thomsen's ideals were reflected in the new director's declaration that his museum must be no mere array of lifeless treasures: 'from the time one senses their implications they are no longer lifeless'. During his time there the collections grew considerably. He had established a purchasing account and organized excavations at, for instance, two of the barrows at Old Uppsala (1846–7) and megalithic tombs in the Falköping area, to mention only a few of his activities. His personal research work was chiefly on numismatics and medieval remains. Among his assistants should be mentioned the able field-worker P. A. Säve, who has left many valuable reports.

56

During these decades, the statutes dealing with field-monuments and archaeological finds underwent some modifications. N. H. Sjöborg, the Professor of History and Archaeology at Lund, used his friendship with the University Chancellor and Minister of State Lars von Engeström to obtain a special appointment as Inspector of State Antiquities. This position, which he took up in 1814, placed him in a kind of irregular relationship to the then Royal Antiquary, while on the other hand he was expected to report to the Vitterhetsakademi. His responsibilities in regard to ancient monuments were 'to ensure, through announcement in the appropriate places, that those which have value are protected, so long as they can be retained without undue encroachment on the rights of the landowner; from which it follows that the landowner is entitled to do whatever he pleases with unscheduled monuments'. Sjöborg went to work on a long series of inspections with a view to issuing protection orders, and also succeeded in restoring the remarkable Bronze Age burial at Kivik, which had lain in a

56 Excavation sketches by P. A. Säve, showing the investigation of a megalithic tomb in Sweden

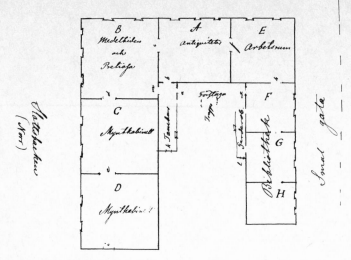

57 Plan of Hildebrand's museum in the Ridderstolpeska House, Stockholm, drawn by Hildebrand himself for C.J. Thomsen

sorry state of disrepair after several of its important picture-stones had been removed and later brought back piecemeal to the site.

Alarmed at the increasing spoliation of ancient monuments, Sjöborg proposed new legislation. Through the support of the Vitterhetsakademi, a decree was issued on 17 April 1828, giving the Academy powers to counter this threat. In the first stages, the shortage of permanent staff to inspect the monuments was overcome by appointing local people as representatives, with full authority to act on behalf of the Academy (i.e. the Royal Antiquary or Sjöborg).

State purchasing rights were now also extended to include finds of wood and stone as well as of gold, silver, copper and base metal. These finds went to the Antikvitetsmuseum, from 1855 known as the Statens historiska museum (State Historical Museum), whose head was the Royal Antiquary. Although there was no real change here from the decrees of 1684, 1734 and 1755, which mentioned 'other rarities', a clear statement that materials without intrinsic value also came under the provisions of the law was thought necessary. Later, however, in 1867, these objects were deleted from the statutes, for the Academy now felt it possessed so many stone artifacts that a special provision was unwarranted. On the other hand, the right was reserved to retain any genuinely rare pieces, including those of stone or wood.

After considerable effort, Hildebrand secured proper accommodation and more adequate grants for his museum. In 1844–5 he 57 was allotted a set of rooms in the Ridderstolpeska House, south-east of the royal palace. Here four exhibition areas were available, one for prehistoric exhibits, another for medieval exhibits and two for the coin collection. In addition, he had a work-room and three rooms for the library. He designed display cases and worked hard putting the collection into shape. The museum was opened to the public on 22 October 1844, and thereafter each Wednesday from noon until three o'clock, though Hildebrand confided to

Thomsen that he was somewhat worried about public reaction and indeed anxious to restrict admission by making a small charge. Be that as it may, the museum was satisfactorily installed in its new home, which it rapidly threatened to outgrow, and its presentation was well organized and interesting.

A remarkable individual, who was very influential outside his own country, was the naturalist Sven Nilsson, a native of Skåne, who was born in 1787 and died in 1883, at Lund, where for many years he had been Professor of Zoology and Director of the Zoological Museum. Interested from an early age in prehistory, he owned a large collection and was an enthusiastic comparative ethnographer and archaeologist. Like Stobaeus before him but without knowing of the older man's work, he sought counterparts to his stone artifacts among the implements of 'savage' peoples in other parts of the world, explaining the Scandinavian artifacts by analogy; with this basis and the use of zoological data he was able to describe primitive types of hunter-fishermen, nomads and farmers. On the kitchen-middens, he followed the thinking of his colleague Steenstrup rather than Worsaae, and also asserted his independence of Thomsen. His distinguished study of the Stone Age, first published in 1834, *Outline of the history of hunting and fishing in Scandinavia*, appeared two years later in an expanded form as *The Original Inhabitants of the Scandinavian North*. A second edition, incorporating his highly individual theory that the Bronze Age resulted from Phoenician colonization came out some thirty years later. According to his thinking south-eastern influences assumed the tangible form of a tribal migration. From such sources as the Kivik cist he adduced evidence of sun-worship, tracing it back to the religion of Phoenicia and Egypt. Almost following in Rudbeck's footsteps, he also found indications in place-names of a Baal-cult in his native Sweden.

In Norway, the Trondheim museum was still functioning, and Christiania (present-day Oslo) also acquired an archaeological collection when, in 1810, the Society for the Benefit of Norway appointed an Antiquities Commission, a sort of counterpart to its namesake in Copenhagen. This small collection passed to the University, which in 1828 placed it under the charge of R. Keyser, then a university lecturer, later a professor. He had visited Thomsen and studied the Copenhagen museum, and on his return home he arranged the collection along three-period system lines.[53]

58

58 The collection of the Antiquities Commission in the original showcases of the University's Antiquities Museum, Oslo, as reconstructed for the hundredth Anniversary in 1911

In Bergen, too, there were those who called for a museum. The bishop, Jacob Neumann, was an active antiquary, and one of Norway's most gifted men, W. F. K. Christie, had been appointed governor of the diocese. In 1825 these two were instrumental in establishing the Bergen museum, for which they proposed a broad range of objectives, and also, four years later, an antiquarian journal known as *Urda*. A building was found to house the collections, but there was no money with which to pay assistants. Meanwhile, the enthusiasm of Neumann and Christie had the effect of encouraging other people with similar interests, and among the rich finds recovered at this period were grave-goods from the barrows at Valder near Ålesund, and Avaldsnes (on the island of Karmøy). The excavation of the barrow at Avaldsnes (carried out in 1834 by the local pastor, at Neumann's instigation) justifiably caused quite a stir.[54] The site was known from Snorri; learned men referred to is as 'the cow barrow' (*Kohøjen*), because in Saint Olaf's saga and elsewhere in the literary tradition a story was told about a king on Avaldsnes who had a sacred cow: the king was buried in one barrow and the cow in the other. In the event, no cow was found, but instead the excavators came upon a rich human burial from the late Roman period, containing gold rings, a sword, glass, bronze vessels and many other objects.

The largest gold ring was purchased by the archaeological collection of the University of Christiania and catalogued by Keyser. The remainder – except for a few valuable pieces – were presented to the Bergen museum. Six gold finger-rings and a gold pin disappeared after being sent back to the rectory at Avaldsnes.

There was strong feeling that this barrow should not have been destroyed, and the artist I. C. Dahl, who knew the spot well and had drawn it, was angered. The experience had the effect of making him the moving spirit, a few years later, in 1845, behind the Society for the Protection of Ancient Monuments in Norway, whose journal has since published numerous reports on prehistoric remains and excavations.

At this point of time Schleswig-Holstein was still attached to the Danish Crown and it was natural for Thomsen to encourage the university city of Kiel to set up a museum. This was not easily accomplished, for although there were several large private collections in the province, in the city itself interest was limited. There was, moreover, a certain hostility toward Danish policies. But in 1834, a museum society was formed called *Die königliche Schleswig-Holstein-Lauenburgische Gesellschaft für die Sammlung und Erhaltung vaterländischer Alterthümer*. Professor Falck, a jurist, was elected chairman and it was directed by the professor of Danish language and literature, Chr. Flor, a specialist in Nordic tradition.[55] The museum incorporated a gift of three hundred objects sent by the Antiquities Commission to the University library, and also a gift from a private collector. Thomsen knew that the Copenhagen museum might suffer through his decision to encourage local collections, but he had by now committed himself to a policy of decentralization. He had previously sent a collection of prehistoric artifacts to Odense, where he wished to see a diocesan museum established. In a letter to Hildebrand he described the ill-feeling which his work for the Kiel museum had aroused in Copenhagen, and which he chose to disregard: 'Here too I met with misgivings; we shall lose ten pieces a year – but, on the other hand, a hundred will be saved for scholarship which were previously quite unknown to us.' His arguments were sound. It was not his fault if progress was slow in Kiel. Falck and Flor were divided by political and personal antagonisms, and some years passed before the museum was organized on a professional basis.

In Finland, a Grand Duchy under the Tsars since 1809, archaeological inquiry was spurred on by the Romantic and nationalist movements.[56] The same trend was evidenced by the Finnish folk-songs and the *Kalevala*. These intellectual currents influenced M. A. Castrén, the founder of Finno-Ugric archaeology. For him it was a natural step to search for archaeological vestiges wherever he found Finnish-speaking people. So, on his journeys through Finland, northern Russia and Siberia, he studied burial-mounds and prehistoric strongholds, describing them in his book, *Travelling in Russian Karelia*, of 1829. In a plea for the investigation of Finland's burial-mounds, published in 1851, he gave an account of the research upon which he had been engaged over the previous decade, contending that these were ancient Finnish monuments.

Important in this connection are his studies of tumuli in the Minusinsk area, some of which he identified as Tatar or Kirghiz and others as Finnish. He realized, however, that it would be necessary to compare the Siberian tumuli more closely with the parallels in Finland, and concluded by saying that it seemed beyond all doubt that the graves found in Finnish territory were the work of the Finns themselves. But did these graves possess anything in common with those in Siberia? If the answer was in the affirmative, one might conclude that the Finnish tribe had its origins in the Altai Mountains, and that they had in earlier times populated European Russia, building there the same kind of monuments as were to be seen in Siberia.

Here Castrén stressed the importance, in attempting to trace the origin of the Finns, of conducting excavations outside as well as inside Finland, in the vast tracts to the east where Finnish was spoken in his time. This was the direction taken by subsequent research.

Chapter Five

Danish Archaeology under Worsaae

59   WHEN Thomsen died in 1865, Worsaae became incontestably the leading figure in Danish archaeology. Since 1847 he had been Inspector for the Conservation of Antiquarian Monuments, while Thomsen was Director of the Royal Museum for Nordic Antiquities.[57] They were both members of the Antiquities Commission, but with the Constitution of 1848 and its attendant changes these two institutions were brought directly under the Ministry of Culture, and the Commission, by now ineffectual, was dissolved. To Worsaae fell the heavy task of protecting Denmark's prehistoric monuments. Both he and the museum were engaged in excavations, but still on a limited scale. For a long time he had to manage without helpers, but there was ready co-operation between the two antiquarian institutions. Worsaae did frequent rounds of inspection in various parts of the country, and when finds came to his notice he passed them on to the museum.

Worsaae's career began promisingly enough. Born in Vejle in 1821, the son of a wealthy official, he developed an interest in archaeological finds while still a schoolboy. In an amazingly short space of time he had purchased an excellent collection, while also conducting excavations and visiting ancient monuments. One of his investigations, undertaken together with an older friend, who was an officer in the army, was at Grønhøj, a megalithic tomb near Horsens.[58] Soldiers assisted them with this heavy work. Digging was going on eagerly when one of the roof-stones collapsed. It might easily have put an end to the career of our youthful scholar, but in the nick of time he scrambled out of the stone chamber, which remained in its ruined state until a recent excavation.

The nationalist and Romantic movements of the period were an inspiration to Worsaae, as he himself puts it in his absorbing memoirs. They added in a special way to the attraction of archaeology.

Newly arrived in Copenhagen in 1838, as a student, he made it his first concern to meet the group of archaeologists at the museum, which was then in Christiansborg. Thomsen and his assistants made him heartily welcome, and he worked with them voluntarily for the next few years. Then, with his father's illness and sudden death, his family fell on hard times. From now on Worsaae would have to fend for himself. It occurred to him that he might solve his difficulties by requesting a salary for his work at the museum, hitherto unpaid. But he failed to reckon with the parsimonious director. Wary of committing himself, Thomsen

59 J.J.A. Worsaae (1821–85)

refused the young man's request; honoraria went instead to other volunteers who had been at the museum longer. Worsaae immediately gave up his work there and found other patrons.

There were undeniable differences in nature and temperament between the two men. Unlike Thomsen, Worsaae was a fluent writer. The critic in him immediately sought an outlet, and the target that first presented itself was a paper by the learned literary historian, N. M. Petersen, on a body found interred in a bog near Vejle. This, Petersen asserted, must be Queen Gunnhildr, the wife of Erik Blood-axe. Tactfully, Worsaae pointed out the weaknesses in the older scholar's arguments.[59] Now twenty-three, he showed equal urbanity in refuting the work of three highly esteemed scholars on the so-called Runamo inscription in Blekinge. He demonstrated point by point that their ingenious interpretation of the 'inscription' was full of howlers, and that in any case these scratches, with their superficial resemblance to runes, were natural and not produced by human agency. It is true that this site, though a celebrated one, mentioned in medieval sources, had aroused suspicion in several quarters, but real proof first came with Worsaae's visit to the area. He took casts of the 'runes' and had accurate reproductions prepared, so furnishing documentation. Support for the journey came from no less a person than King Christian VIII, who had taken a liking to the bright young scholar. When he presented the paper to His Majesty, Worsaae was urged not to rest content with destructive criticism but to try to make his own contribution. Scarcely was his visitor out of the room, however, than the king surrendered to whole-hearted

60

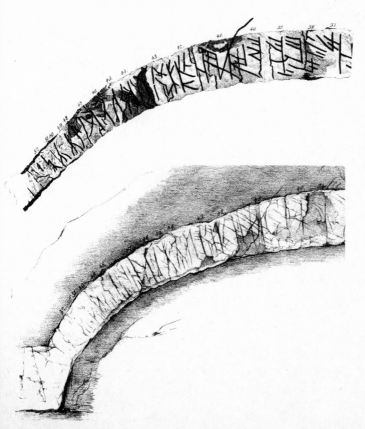

60 Part of the supposed runic inscription at Runamo in Blekinge, Sweden, (a) as published by three Danish scholars in 1841; (b) as correctly reproduced by Worsaae

61 Lundbye's illustration of a
runddysse in Worsaae's *Danmarks
Oldtid*

amusement at the startling revelation. Being deeply interested in archaeology himself, he realized that the conclusions of the paper must be correct, and decided to take the young archaeologist under his wing.

It was not long before Worsaae had produced the original contribution which the king had called for. He was asked to write a short survey of the early history of Denmark, and the result was his *Primeval Antiquities of Denmark*, first published in 1843 (English edition, London 1849) – a small book which was to prove epoch-making in its grasp of the subject and its lucidity of style. Seven thousand copies were distributed, an unusually large number. The attractive illustrations included two woodcuts of grave-mounds by Lundbye. The content was roughly the same as in Thomsen's guide-book, but more compellingly presented. Worsaae's treatment was for the most part based on Thomsen's results, but in a couple of passages he lent his material a topical slant. The book opens boldly with a sentence which recalled Vedel's words, two centuries earlier:

61

'It is inconceivable that a nation which cares about itself and its independence could rest content without reflecting on its past.'

He went through the various types of prehistoric monuments and artifacts, using Thomsen's three-period system but proposing a more elaborate chronology. His conception of the significance of prehistory was shaped partly by rational considerations and partly by the Romanticist notion of a close link between the modern Dane and his prehistoric forbears, of a harmony between the grave-mounds and the countryside.

'It is in this way that the relics of prehistory strengthen our links with the Fatherland. We enter, through them, into a more lively empathy with hills and valleys, fields and pastures; for it is through the burial-mounds that lie humped up on their surfaces and through the prehistoric artifacts which have lain safely, down through the centuries, in their recesses, that the land can constantly remind us of the fact that our fathers, a free, independent people, have dwelt from time immemorial in this country; more, they command us to look to our heritage, to resist foreign domination over a soil that shields our fathers' bones and in which our most sacred and venerable memories are rooted.'

There is the ring of the young Grundtvig about this powerful pronouncement. It was a timely message, in the 1840s, for the Danish public. Everyone was expectantly awaiting a decisive trial of strength between the opposed policies of Denmark and Schleswig-Holstein, and in this atmosphere of heightened nationalism Worsaae's words made a great impact. We shall encounter them later in modern Danish history. Worsaae's little book was really brilliant propaganda for archaeology, which he constantly links with a number of wider issues – historical, national, ethnic, not to mention the questions of excavation technique and conservation – presenting it to the reader as a new field of study. This book represented a pioneering contribution, and the ideas it contained were widely disseminated through the English and German translations, which gave it importance outside Denmark.

Worsaae's next few years were occupied with extensive study-tours and productive investigations. The king had not forgotten his talented protégé, and it was through his good offices that Worsaae was able to travel round Britain and Ireland in 1846–7, studying remains from the Viking occupations. The outcome was the book titled *Remains of the Danes and the Norsemen in England, Scotland and Ireland.* An acute observer, he was struck by the correspondence between certain ornaments and weapons in the British Isles and the Scandinavian finds; he acquired examples of these types and sent them back to the Copenhagen museum, with the object of documenting the contacts and demonstrating that the artifacts were identical.

This is an amazingly mature, fluently written book. Worsaae draws on the entire range of sources – literature, archaeology, coins, place-names, inscriptions and many others – and out of this heterogeneous material assembles a balanced exposition, not to be superseded until our own times. It represents archaeology in the original, broad sense of the word, but its strength lies in Worsaae's independent observations. He had an acute eye for significant detail. An instance is the way he interprets the ornamented rune-stones on the Isle of Man. He shows that only Scandinavian masters could have carved the characteristic stone crosses. The language of the runes was Norse, and the decoration had close parallels in Scandinavia. There was an important inscription naming Gaut as the first maker of crosses on the Isle of Man. Worsaae was quite clear that the models for stones with crosses were not Scandinavian, but it must, he argued, have been Scandinavians who 'left the imprint of their highly-individual and inventive imaginations in this distinctive ornamentation'. All in all, the book contains numerous independent and reliable conclusions: by way of summing up he points to the remains he has discussed as proof that the prehistoric Scandinavians were not barbaric savages but an artistic and culturally advanced people.

Arriving home, Worsaae was soon appointed Inspector for the Conservation of Antiquarian Monuments, a position which placed heavy demands on him but which also led to important undertakings. In 1848 he was attached to a commission supported by the Royal Society, formed for the purpose of investigating the shell-mounds.[60] In Zealand, heaps of oyster shells containing flint artifacts had been observed to lie inland from the modern shoreline. It seemed likely that these accumulations of shells marked the original position of the coastline, and hence it was important to know to what period these artifacts could be attributed. The investigation was promoted by two scientists, the geologist Forchhammer, who had crossed swords with Worsaae during the Runamo controversy, and the zoologist Steenstrup, who had studied bog stratification, demonstrating changes in prehistoric animal and plant life through finds in the different layers. Working partly independently, partly in collaboration – an interesting example of co-operation between science and archaeology – the three scholars set about their investigation. The nature of the shell-heaps first became clear with Worsaae's excavation of an example near Mejlgaard, in east Jutland. How he arrived at his interpretation can be seen from the entry in his diary for 24 September 1851. While removing part of the heap for road-fill, the proprietor had noticed a great number of antiquities and called in Worsaae, who was engaged on an official round of inspection in Jutland.

The heap, situated somewhat inland and slightly raised above the flat coastal strip, consisted, as Worsaae noted, of a vast quantity of oyster shells, together with mussels, cockles and winkles. There were traces of charcoal all over the site.

'As I wanted to establish for myself, if possible, that man-made objects were in fact to be found underneath these layers of oyster shells, I proceeded to remove a whole section of the pile, to a depth of about five feet below the surface. Down to this level the shells lay quite firmly packed in layers. Right amongst the oyster shells I was fortunate enough to make my first find, the tip of an antler, which had clearly been carved with a sharp instrument. Then came a small bone, which bore equally unmistakable signs of having been carved. Hoping to find more, my assistants and I continued at the same spot, stripping further portions of the bank down to the same depth, and soon I was overjoyed to find an axe, or so-called adze, rough-hewn from flint, together with assorted animal bones, some charcoal, and so on – all of these finds in different positions, scattered among the shells.'

Worsaae compared this shell-heap with other sites, noted that the finds included coarse potsherds, and concluded with what he termed a conjectural interpretation:

'Bearing in mind that oysters cannot be traced anywhere in the area round Mejlgaard except for precisely this pile that I have described, which is clearly delimited, and that artifacts were found scattered throughout it along with charcoal and animal bones, one cannot help supposing that in early prehistoric times, when the shoreline lay closer to this bank, there must have been a kind of eating-place here for the local population. This would explain the cooking vessels, charcoal, animal bones, and flint blades (for oyster-opening).'

This day-book brings us into direct contact with a brilliant research-worker. From his observations he draws logical and precise conclusions. His associates in the project took note of his new approach to the problem, and Steenstrup adopted it as his own. He too examined the finds of bones, using them as a source of information on animal life.

These new developments caused excitement among contemporary scholars. Thomsen accepted Worsaae's observations, realizing their far-reaching implications, but others were sceptical. With time, however, Worsaae felt confirmed in his conclusions, and these shell-heaps came to be known as 'Kjøkkenmøddinger' ('kitchen-middens'). This apt expression became widely adopted in archaeological terminology and because of its picturesqueness was taken over unchanged by other languages. It became one of the few Danish words to achieve international currency.

Worsaae was positive that finds from the kitchen-middens belonged to a culture different from the one which produced the artifacts found in megalithic burials. The following statement, written in 1859, puts forward this view: 'In oyster-heaps flint tools are generally of a special, extremely crude type, the pottery too is very crude, and one finds a special sort of bone artifact in relatively large numbers; whereas the flint tools, stone objects, pottery, amber ornaments, and so on in megalithic burials are much more developed and show a different method of manufacture.' He placed the two find-groups in different periods, the Early and Late Stone Age respectively. In his illustrated manual of prehistoric artifacts from Scandinavia, published in 1854, he showed these two groups, as well as two different classes from the Iron Age, one early and one late. The Bronze Age was also broken up into an early period with inhumation and a later one with cremation.

Originally (in *Danmarks Oldtid*) Worsaae had suggested that the Scandinavian Iron Age was a brief phase rounding off the prehistoric era, but in the course of time he recognized that it clearly reached back much further. Some Roman imports, which he published in 1849,[61] attested contact with the Roman Empire in the first centuries A D, and since they occurred together with Iron Age grave-goods they could be used for dating purposes. It was not, however, until 1853, with the discovery at Vimose (Funen) of a large votive offering of weapons, which he and Herbst together examined, that he expressed his views in a positive manner. In 1865, simultaneously with Engelhardt, he postulated that the Iron Age consisted of three periods, the first from A D 200 to 300 to *c.* 450, a second from *c.* 450 to *c.* 700, and a third from *c.* 700 to *c.* 1000.[62] This put the beginning of the Iron Age rather later than previously assumed. For the first period he used as a basis the large new weapon-finds which had been recovered from bogs, in particular the Torsbjerg (Schleswig) find. The second find-group was made up of coins and gold objects which could be dated from the fifth to the seventh century. The third group consisted of Viking-period types, which could be identified with certainty.

62 Neolithic stone implements, (a) Early Stone Age flint axe; (b) late Stone Age polished flint axe (after Worsaae)

At this productive stage of his studies, Worsaae was also attached to the University. In 1855 he became the first academic teacher of Prehistory in Scandinavia. In 1866, however, he resigned from this post on succeeding Thomsen at the museum, while continuing to serve as Director of Ancient Monuments. The result was increased co-ordination between the two institutions, since there was also some overlapping among the staff.

In spite of the disastrous defeat of 1864 and the cuts in the State budget, Worsaae's authoritative standing and gift for diplomacy ensured the implementation of a plan toward which he had long been working and which required the co-operation of all archaeologists. In 1873 the Rigsdag approved an annual grant of no less than 3500 dollars for the inspection and eventual protection of

63 The archaeologists J. B. Løffler (seated) and Henry Petersen at Hennetved in 1875, equipped for their survey work with straw hats and shoulder bags

prehistoric monuments in Denmark.[63] This was the first systematic survey of prehistoric monuments attempted by any country, and the members of the staff carried it through competently and enthusiastically. An area was assigned to each archaeologist who, together with a draughtsman, carried out a thorough inspection. In some districts, where there were exceptionally well-informed local people available, it was possible to delegate the work of inspection. Gradually a body of information on finds and field-monuments was gathered, information which has subsequently proved invaluable, though it was not in all cases followed up with more thorough inspections and investigations in later years. In his account of this work, Worsaae explained the ideas behind the plan and the means by which it was implemented; in translation, his paper attracted wide interest abroad.

A second scheme which Worsaae had been trying to put into effect for many years he returned to in 1866; this was the creation of provincial inspectorates, to take charge of antiquarian work. It was clear to him that the central protection authority which he headed could never hope for State grants sufficient to cover its many responsibilities. He, therefore, sent letters to the boards of the newly established museums in Odense, Aalborg, Viborg,

Aarhus, Ribe and Reykjavik, calling for a 'Commission [of the Trustees] for the preservation of ancient monuments in the diocese' and also for the appointment of a provincial inspector, to be paid by the administration.[64] Unfortunately, nothing came of this sensible suggestion, which would have divided the country into convenient working units (dioceses) of approximately equal size. Instead, it was chance alone that fixed the working areas of the new museums, and the fortunes of prehistoric monuments continued, as heretofore, to be dependent on goodwill.

At this time Worsaae was also engaged in a thorough reorganization of the collections in the Prince's Palace, where the exhibitions, especially the prehistoric section, were newly arranged to conform with current scientific opinion. He was naturally the central figure at the international congress of archaeologists in Copenhagen in 1869, where the official programme included an excursion to the kitchen-middens at Sølager. During his brief term as Minister for Education and Ecclesiastical Affairs (1874–5) he showed a flair for administration. This active and successful man died suddenly in 1885, still occupied with schemes which depended on his influence for their fulfilment.

Worsaae had a sure grasp of the problems that presented themselves. His lucidity of thought and brilliant intellect were responsible, in large measure, for a breadth of achievement unrivalled by his contemporaries. His significance, from a scientific viewpoint, lies in the prominence he gave to material evidence in archaeology, whether prehistoric artifacts or field-monuments. He stood firmly by his opinions, critical or constructive. He knew well that his lively imagination could lead him to put forward far-fetched theories; but, in any case, he liked being provocative. With his wide knowledge of finds in other countries, he was well equipped for comparative studies, and we see this expertise at work in his later papers. He had a winning personality. Those who visited the Old Nordic museum tell about an active institution, with a healthy spirit of co-operation but with room, too, for differences of opinion. A note of enthusiasm was evident, a conscious wish to contribute and to ensure that one's efforts received recognition.

One member of this talented and hard-working staff was Conrad Engelhardt, the result of whose excavation led to a better understanding of such subjects as Iron Age chronology. Engelhardt's father, a shipbroker, died young, and Thomsen, a friend of the family, looked after the child, providing him with an education and later taking him on as private secretary.[65] Engelhardt was one of the company at Thomsen's bachelor rooms in Dronningens Tvaergade, where the young archaeologists used to gather, but he felt no particular enthusiasm for archaeology. He first developed a deeper interest in it after a journey to Italy with Thomsen and Herbst, and from then on he concerned himself with finds that established contact with the Roman Empire. He competently carried through a series of investigations which yielded good results. He was at first based at Flensburg, where he was appointed lecturer and Director of the Royal Collection of Nordic Antiquities. This modest institution, which had been set up in 1852 as a counterpart to the Kiel museum, assumed a leading place

64 C. Engelhardt (1825–81)

thanks to the efforts of Engelhardt. Just at this time, objects of amazing richness, including weapons and Roman imports, were recovered from two bogs, at Torsbjerg in Angel and Nydam in 65 Sundeved. The Torsbjerg finds, which passed to the museum in 1856, prompted Engelhardt to start an investigation, which continued until 1861. In 1859 he extended this work to Nydam, where he carried on until the outbreak of war in 1863. On account of the war this excavation was performed at frantic speed, in an effort to rescue the large oak boat and other important finds. The eminent draughtsman Magnus Petersen lent his assistance, arriving in November and drawing as much as he could: Engelhardt then packed the priceless finds in crates, thirty-two in all. They were brought to a rectory on Als, and from there secretly conveyed by steamship to Korsør.

With the peace of October 1865 Denmark was obliged to guarantee the return of these valuable finds to Schleswig-Holstein, but this was only done when the Germans for their part had paid a reward of twenty-five thousand marks to a person who located the site. These bog-finds were considered so important that they became an issue in the dispute between the two countries.

The publication of the south Jutland bog-finds proceeded in spite of these vicissitudes. Engelhardt was given a post at the Copenhagen museum. He now turned to the investigation of new

65 These finds from Torsbjerg bog, and in particular the shield boss bearing the Roman inscription *Aelius Aelianus*, played an important part in the discussion on the existence of an early Iron Age

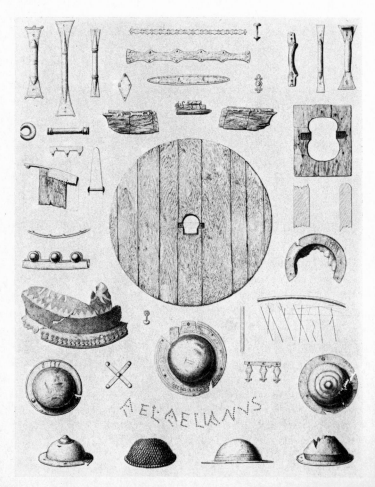

weapon-finds from bogs, in particular the find from Vimose, on Funen. He also studied rich Iron Age burial-places in Zealand, together with the Bronze Age barrow known as Borum Eshøj, which we shall consider presently. He toured extensively in Jutland and Lolland and, with Magnus Petersen, mapped pre-historic remains for Worsaae's survey. He published the Iron Age bog-finds with some care, but their interpretation as votive offer-ings was due to Worsaae, that indefatigable scholar. Public recog-nition came with an honorary doctorate, conferred at the Jubilee of the University of Copenhagen in 1879; two years later, Engelhardt died, energetic and indomitable to the last.

Borum Eshøj was a well-preserved oak-coffin burial. It and similar examples had already been known from accidental finds but were now subjected to a thorough investigation, which yielded important results.[66] In 1860 Fladhøj and Hvidding in south-west Jutland were excavated, and in the following year the near-by Trindhøj and Store Kongehøj. Borum Eshøj was un-covered in 1871, and later the Jutland sites of Muldbjerg, Bredhøj and Guldhøj, the last-named in 1891. At all these sites the archaeologists went about their work with meticulous care. They were assisted by draughtsmen and sometimes also by specialists in anatomy, and even the camera was used in these archaeological investigations. Photographs give a vivid impression of the workers and the finds themselves. The telegraph was used to call in experts, since time was scarce and interest keen. The water which had preserved the organic remains had been prevented from seeping away by a hard pan in the ground beneath the interment, and a similar impervious layer had formed above it. It was re-cultivation of the land that led to the discovery of these informative sites. Fresh light was shed on Bronze Age culture by the clothing in particular, though also by articles of wood and horn.

66–68

Engelhardt described the investigation of one of the burials in a couple of letters to Worsaae, the first dated 2 August 1875:

'An oak coffin just discovered in Borum Eshøj. Stones packed round it; both ends have been freed and water is streaming out of it.' [On 7 August the lid was taken off:] 'At 2 p.m. yesterday the coffin was opened, before a large crowd of people. Inside lay the best preserved skeleton I have seen, clothed in a tunic which had been held together by a (corroded) leather belt with a well-preserved wooden button. In the left arm, which was crooked, rested a finely-ornamented wooden scabbard, but our expecta-tions of a bronze sword were disappointed, since – oddly enough – the scabbard contained only a bronze dagger, the hilt of which was preserved. The right arm was stretched out alongside the body. Remains of a wide leather baldric hung over the right shoulder. Under the left shoulder a bone comb, in good condition, the upper part transparent. To the right side of the head and a little above it a well-preserved box of wooden chips, with lid. All this covered by a flowing shroud of woollen material, and above that again an animal hide (from an ox?) with the sides tucked in under the body. Traces of sandals by the feet.'

These concise sentences suggest hasty composition and an intense concern for precision. This was Engelhardt's one chance to inspect

66 The excavation of the Guldhøj barrow, directed by V. Boye in 1891 during very inclement weather. The wind and the cold have given the workers themselves a rather Bronze Age look! This is one of the earliest occasions on which photography was used to document an excavation

67 The Guldhøj cist is opened and its contents revealed: among them, a folding chair and wooden vessels

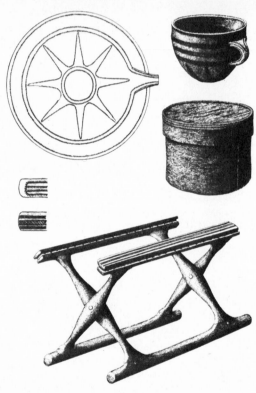

68 Boye's publication of the Guldhøj cist included this careful illustration of some of the most distinctive finds

an untouched relic of Bronze Age culture; it was essential to make the most of the opportunity. It was finds like the one at Borum Eshøj that would make the Old Nordic museum famous. The draughtsman stood by to record details, and the rare find was sent off carefully for further treatment. Section drawings and plans were naturally also prepared.

On other sites, too, competent archaeologists were at work. On Bornholm, Herbst had investigated early Iron Age burials north of Rønne. Engelhardt came here several years later, studying rich burials near Gudhjem. The island's new county prefect,

E. Vedel, appointed in 1866, soon developed an interest in archaeology.[67] He noticed some dark pits in gravel diggings and, after a closer investigation, realized that they represented the remains of funeral pyres. For many years to follow these and numerous other prehistoric remains were his favourite concern. He began thorough investigations at Kanegaard, near Rønne, and continued at Kannikegaard in Bodilsker, where the labour force of the farm was placed at his disposal. During 1869 he excavated six hundred of these burials. His results were published the following year in *Aarbøger for Nordisk Oldkyndighed* (Journal of Northern Antiquity and History). The investigation of cremation-pits and skeleton burials at the Kannikegaard site was not completed until 1876, but in the intervening period Vedel produced a tentative analysis of early Iron Age chronology, published in the 1872 volume of *Aarbøger*. The study provides evidence of his methodical habits. He needed only to make a few corrections to the contents of his note-books, in which he also drew burials and important finds and mounted photographs, which he used frequently to record finds. In this way his note-books became a good basis for his studies after the finds themselves had been sent off to Copenhagen.

69 E. Vedel (1824–1909)

71

Vedel had observed that the finds at the Kannikegaard burial-ground were distributed in a characteristic fashion. Their incidence clearly reflected a gradual change in the interments from one end of the long gravel bank to the other. It would be possible, therefore, to reach chronological conclusions from the distribution of the finds. Having by now investigated 1,550 cremation-pits, he also had available a substantial amount of comparative material from other sites. He divided the graves into three groups.

70

The first class contained, among other things, belt-hooks, bent pins, and iron brooches 'with the point bent back'. These types appeared at Kanegaard and at Mandhøj, a related burial-site. Cairns also occurred at both sites. The few examples of this class at Kannikegaard were clustered to the north of the cemetery. In Vedel's view, it ante-dates the Roman influence evident in the second class, and the brooches had early Swiss parallels.

72

The second class, containing ribbon-shaped and 'humped' fibulae, finely executed pottery, Roman glass beads and much besides, was distributed over an area south of the early interments at Kannikegaard.

The third class had numerous counterparts in the large weapon-finds of Vimose, Nydam, Torsbjerg and elsewhere, for instance in fibula-forms and the presence of two-edged swords. This group had an extensive distribution area still farther to the south.

Noting the find at the south end of Kannikegaard of a grave containing a chip-carved zoomorphic fibula of the 'Middle Iron Age' – Worsaae's term for the period which on Bornholm was characterized by late Roman gold coins (fifth to beginning of the sixth century) and other typical finds – Vedel conjectured that the cremation-pit period ante-dated the year 400. He also deduced that it must have been a very lengthy period, since it was clear to him that the numerous burials which he had excavated must constitute no more than a fraction of the original total, which he

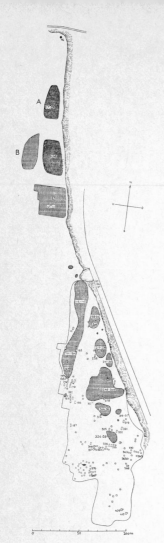

70 The Kannikegaard burial-ground, on Bornholm (after E. Vedel). The oldest graves (to the north) are indicated by a darker tint

71 Page 147 of Vedel's excavation note-book

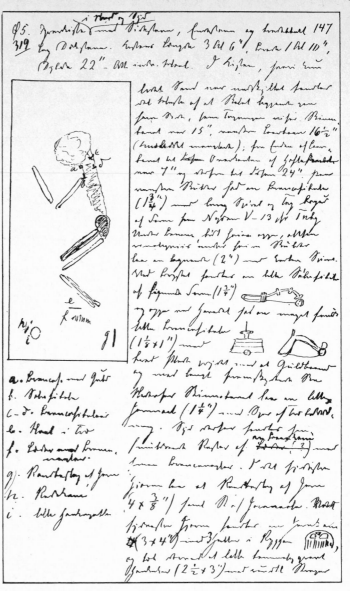

estimated at forty to fifty thousand. Just how long it had been he attempted to work out from an article on population growth in Denmark. He estimated that in AD 400 Bornholm had a population of 4,200, and by dividing the total interred in cremation-pits into generations Vedel arrived at 100 BC as a beginning-point for the period. The cairns at Kanegaard and Mandhøj contained iron pins of still earlier types; three-quarters of the cairns belonged to the Iron Age, while the remainder contained Bronze Age objects. This led Vedel to the conclusion that the beginning of the Iron Age may have been even earlier, 'perhaps three or four centuries before the birth of Christ'. Such a hypothesis agreed well with the presence of Roman imports (glass beads, bronzes, etc.) in the second class of cremation-pits as compared with the absence of them in the first class. On the other hand, the bulk of finds in the second class was plainly of local origin – the pottery showed that. Roman imports were particularly well represented in the third class, in the shape, for instance, of bronze vessels and glass. In spite of foreign influence on such things as ornaments, Vedel felt that tradition was the chief factor and that the immigrations were ephemeral in character. It seemed most likely to have been the 'Nordic and Norse-speaking people who have lived on this island, at least since the beginning of the Bronze Age, that is to say, probably much in excess of a thousand years before Christ'.

The paper opened up new perspectives, and most of its arguments were accepted, but the chronology itself met with scepticism. The first criticism, from Sweden, was voiced by Hans Hildebrand, son of B. E. Hildebrand: he accepted Vedel's system of classes and laid emphasis on the contact with Gotland, whose early Iron Age artifacts became more explicable when connected with Vedel's finds, but disputed Vedel's early dating.[68] In subsequent articles Vedel reverted to a more conservative estimate – and the same may be observed of other attempts at a chronology at this period in Denmark – but he returned to the question in a book summarizing his work on Bornholm, *Bornholm Oldtidsminder og Oldsager*, published in 1886, and especially in the postscript he wrote for this book in 1897.

The rich finds from the later Iron Age proved particularly significant. The Middle Iron Age was now more closely delimited, through the arrangement of characteristic types in series showing which belonged together and were contemporary.

Another expert on the prehistoric remains of his own area who made a pioneering contribution to archaeology was the owner of the estate of Broholm (Funen), F. Sehested. He was responsible for a number of successful excavations, and published his findings in two volumes. Of great importance were his interesting experiments in prehistoric technique. People who visited the hospitable manor house give a sympathetic portrait of the energetic nobleman and underline the owner's practical grasp of how to go about testing prehistoric tools.[69] One of his projects was to build a log cabin. Flint axes were fitted with hafts, and then the carpenters chopped down forty-eight trees, each eight

72 Pre-Roman Iron Age artifacts found on Bornholm. (a) Iron belt fastener; (b) iron brooch (after E. Vedel)

73 The wooden house at Broholm (Funen), which Sehested built with Stone Age implements

inches thick. It took only eight minutes for two men to fell a tree of this size, and the axes suffered no ill effects. For the job of building, axes, adzes, mortise chisels, gouges, etc., all of flint, were used. Altogether, it took the workers, who of course were unused to the techniques involved, sixty-six days to complete the cabin, which was 14 feet long by 12 feet wide and had a thatched roof. Other experiments were conducted, for example polishing flint axes by six different methods and boring a hole into a stone in fourteen different ways.

The prestige of archaeology and its rapid progress in Denmark at the middle of the nineteenth century must in part be attributed to the authoritative stand of Worsaae and his ability to lend the subject topical and general interest. Also important, though, were the numerous rich finds, which aroused general interest. A number of gifted and energetic researchers were at work, among them King Frederik VII. He carried out excavations personally, and his experience went back to his youthful years at Jaegerspris. Later, he was instrumental in starting some large-scale excavations, as in 1861, when, with the assistance of sappers, the barrows at Jelling were investigated. On another occasion he dug with Worsaae and Steenstrup in the Mejlgaard kitchen-midden, in order to determine which of the two specialists was correct in the

73

74 The excavation of the royal tumulus at Jelling, Jutland (1861). *Top*: Soldiers drilling down to find the grave. Worsaae, in his uniform as Director of Antiquities, explains the procedure to King Frederik VII, who is visiting the site. *Bottom*: Worsaae and the king studying the finds, with the king's consort, Countess Danner, near by. (Drawn by J. Kornerup)

dating of the finds. Each persisted unshaken in his opinion:
Steenstrup maintained that the kitchen-middens and the megalithic
burials belonged to the same period, while Worsaae for his part
noted with satisfaction that the site had revealed not a single piece
of polished flint, a result which in his view confirmed the idea of
two periods, the kitchen-middens being earlier than the megalithic
burials. In the same year the king began investigations of barrows
containing oak coffins, meeting the expenses himself. Such was his
enthusiasm that on one occasion he called the archaeologists out
in the depths of December, when a new coffin was discovered.
They were successful, though, in postponing the excavations
until the weather improved. The king was not afraid of exerting
himself, working eagerly and with good humour, and sometimes
amusing himself at the expense of his fellow-workers. But he was
generous as well. The expenditure for one excavation totalled
115 dollars and 13 shillings, of which rather more than three
dollars went in telegrams to the king. The money was paid without
hesitation.

The king published an interesting paper on the construction of
the 'Giants' Graves' which was translated into many languages.
First put forward in an address to the Oldskriftsselskab, of which
he was president, on 29 May 1857 at Christiansborg, his theories
were based on his own observations – such as the use, for instance,
of fire to break up boulders, a technique employed in his day by
village stone-masons (and confirmed by recent experiments). The
stones, he thought, would have been transported by using tree-
trunks as rollers. The construction of a temporary earth ramp
would enable the roof-stones to be rolled into position above the
chamber. His excavation reports, partly prepared by a personal
attendant, who shared his interest in archaeology, are very useful;
but even he had difficulty in winning acceptance for his favourite
ideas, such as cannibalism in the Stone Age, though the evidence
was good enough. He held to his opinions.

75 King Frederik VII supervising
soldiers at work on a barrow on
Skodsborg, north Zealand.
(Drawing by J. Magnus
Petersen)

Chapter Six

Scandinavian Dialogue: Montelius and Müller

In the latter half of the nineteenth century and the beginning of the twentieth, Scandinavian archaeology was dominated by two great scholars, men who were diverse in intellect and stature but matched each other in their depth of learning and creativity. Oscar
76 Montelius, the grand and imperturbable Swede, was one of the few archaeologists we might fairly describe as a genius;[70] his
78 Danish counterpart, Sophus Müller, was trenchant and original, as acute in observation as in repartee.[71] They were reserved in their personal dealings with each other, but each found the writings of the other stimulating and an incentive for fruitful criticism. Without this rivalry neither would probably have achieved such brilliant results. In their own countries each of them was surrounded by a lively circle of scholars.

Montelius' thinking was shaped, as a young man, by the natural
77 sciences: like his contemporary Hans Hildebrand he was indirectly inspired by Darwin's theories. Müller had a classical education and moved on rapidly to an appointment at the Old Nordic Museum (later called the National Museum), which became a part of his life. Its administration was as much a concern to him as academic research. Publication, preparation of finds for exhibition or storage, and a multiplicity of antiquarian duties – excavations, inspections, conservation – all were taken care of by this sound but demanding institution. Young archaeologists received their training here. In return, Müller had full access to the museum's rich collections and its resources of staff and excavation results.

Montelius was more of a free agent. He was in a better position to study and travel. Hans Hildebrand had succeeded his father as Royal Antiquary in 1879, and Montelius occupied a post at the Statens historiska museum (State Historical Museum) until he in turn succeeded Hildebrand at the age of sixty-four. Throughout this long period he was a loyal and tactful assistant to Hildebrand, accepting frequent engagements as a lecturer. Müller, who in 1872 became co-director of the newly constituted National Museum, was inhibited in social contact by increasing deafness, but he too had a gift for popularizing his ideas, more perhaps as a writer than as a speaker.

Oscar Montelius was the older of the two; he was born on 9 September 1843 in the Stockholm house where he lived until his death on 4 November 1921. He typified Stockholm, just as Müller did Copenhagen, and his interest in history went back to his childhood. His father was a friend of the older Hildebrand,

76 Oscar Montelius (1843–1921)

and when father and son together visited the Old Nordic Museum they passed on a message of goodwill from him to Thomsen.

So it was that Oscar Montelius and Hans Hildebrand were childhood friends, and both later spent their student years at Uppsala. Hildebrand was the first to take his doctorate, with a monograph on the early ethnography of Sweden, while Montelius based his dissertation, titled *From the Iron Age* (1869), on the discussion of a number of controversial finds. He was convinced that the conventional date for the beginning of the Iron Age, the second century AD, was too late. Meeting at the international congress of archaeologists in Bologna in 1871, which each of them attended as part of extensive study-tours, they put forward the results of a line of thought that was related to Darwin's theory of evolution. They applied these results to the classification of prehistoric artifacts, calling the method typology. The most thorough exposition of the method we owe to Montelius. In 1873 he produced a study of Bronze Age material from northern and central Sweden, distinguishing an early and a late period through typological series of such artifacts as swords, hanging vessels and brooches. Both he and Hildebrand devoted special attention to this type of ornament, and the same year saw the publication of the latter's *Contribution to the history of the brooch*, the fruit of exhaustive museum studies. In this work an exceedingly diverse array of objects is classified according to types and geo-graphical distribution. By taking both the Scandinavian and the continental European material into consideration, he was able, among other things, to demonstrate how Early Iron Age types in the North originated in the Celtic forms of central Europe. All in all, his work led to a better understanding of the relationship between native Scandinavian typological series and those of other regions, and it was in this connection that Hildebrand criticized Vedel's dating, while accepting that scholar's basic ideas.

The new upsurge in excavation throughout Europe saw major advances in archaeology. To keep abreast of his subject, an

77 Hans Hildebrand, wearing the official uniform of *riksantikvarie* adorned with the Swedish grand cross, inspects excavation work at the prehistoric fortification of Ismanstorp in 1904, in the company of Miss Elsa Auten

archaeologist needs an eye for detail and the opportunity to travel; he should be able to visit places where important new finds are being made. In this respect Montelius was well placed, not being so tied down as Hildebrand. He spent part of each year away from Stockholm, combing museums for material, especially for new finds. The monographs which he published in the following decades were of the greatest value in that they applied not only to Scandinavian archaeology but to other parts of Europe as well. In 1880 his *Brooches from the Bronze Age* superseded the first section of Hildebrand's book. Expressly described as a typological study, it drew on the vastly more extensive body of material now to hand in Greece and Italy. Indifferent to nationalistic considerations, which dictated the scope of archaeological activity in many countries, he made full use of this important background material in his discussion of the Bronze Age in Scandinavia. His *On the dating of the Bronze Age, particularly in relation to Scandinavia*, published in 1885, is a classic in the field of archaeology. The carefully argued form it takes can in part be attributed to his exchange of views on the subject with Müller, and before we examine the work it seems appropriate to introduce the Danish scholar.

Sophus Müller, born 24 May 1846, was a son of the numismatist Ludvig Müller, Director of the Royal Coin Cabinet, which became part of the National Museum. His son was, therefore, at home in a circle which was dominated by the brilliant intellect of Worsaae. He was naturally an admirer of the older scholar, and his memorial oration at the time of Worsaae's death is a fine testimony to his affection.

Müller was then thirty-nine years old and very much the rising star. His expectations, however, were deferred, for Herbst, now sixty-seven, was made Director of the Old Nordic Museum and Müller was promoted to the post of Inspector which Herbst had vacated. In 1892, after long deliberation, the museum was completely restructured. The museums in the Prince's Palace were merged to form the National Museum, which was divided into two departments. Müller became Director of the first of these, which was chiefly concerned with Danish prehistory; the historical period came under the auspices of the second department.

78 Sophus Müller (1846–1934)

Apart from an expedition to Greece and a few other journeys, Müller devoted all his energies to the rich collections of the National Museum. He was convinced that a central museum, containing all objects of scientific interest, was the best answer to the needs of research. He strove single-mindedly to consolidate his museum's special position and to keep the regional museums to the understanding (already reached with those in Aarhus in 1860/61 and Viborg in 1861) that objects of scientific note must be passed on to the Old Nordic Museum. This arrangement was codified in a ministerial proclamation of 1887, in connection with a scheme of subsidies for the local museums. Müller's position was clearly expressed in this document. He wanted the Old Nordic Museum to have supervisory powers over all archaeological collections and to advise on such matters as purchases and exhibitions: the museums could devote limited funds to excavations, but such work must be directed or in any event supervised by the

Old Nordic Museum, which would also have the right to decide which institution should receive the finds.

These restrictive measures naturally aroused some resentment, and there was a decline in the archaeological work of local museums. Worsaae's more liberal policies might well have led to greater decentralization. On the other hand, the contents of the National Museum's exhibition and store-rooms reached impressive proportions and were of high quality.

The conservation authority for prehistoric monuments was incorporated partly into the first, partly into the second department of the National Museum, which thus came to carry the entire responsibility for antiquarian work; also the law of Danefae was administered by the museum. To the Director of the Department of Prehistory was assigned a wide range of duties enabling him to exert considerable influence, a state of affairs which admirably suited a man of Müller's calibre, despite the nagging presence of certain problems, such as an increasing lack of space.

Müller at one time taught archaeology at the University, a task which Worsaae had carried out until 1866. However, he soon gave this up because of pressure of other work, possibly too on account of certain differences of opinion. Academic instruction was, therefore, another feature of archaeology which was brought under the auspices of the National Museum.

Choosing a problem much debated at the time, the Early Iron Age, Müller began his scholarly activities in 1874 with an important article in *Aarbøger for Nordisk Oldkyndighed* (hereafter referred to as *Aarbøger*) in which he carried through a detailed classification of the relevant material; he concluded that there were two phases, corresponding respectively to the early and late Roman periods. But, contrary to Engelhardt who had seen the large bog-finds as representing the beginning of the Iron Age in Denmark, he placed these finds in his second phase. He dismissed Vedel's far-sighted theories of a pre-Roman phase and ignored the new ideas advanced in the previous year by Hans Hildebrand.

Finally, in 1876, Müller entered into real controversy – this time with Montelius – through an article he had written for the same journal. Here he took issue with the division of the Bronze Age into constituent periods, advancing instead the working hypothesis that variations in Bronze Age finds were due to regional differences; there were eastern and western forms, he argued, and the culture areas they represented possessed traditions going back to the Stone Age. The burial customs, too, he explained as two regionally diffused forms. In addition to these arguments, he pointed out differences in men's and women's personal belongings and made a special category of the finds from fields or bogs.

This article had unexpected repercussions. Reviewing Montelius' book, a Swedish historian cited Müller as evidence that the chronological subdivision of the Bronze Age was incorrect. He concluded with the flat statement that Montelius' results had become obsolete before publication – an odd, but not unparalleled, attitude among reviewers. These words so rankled with Montelius, who normally steered clear of polemics, that he devoted the ensuing years to marshalling proof upon proof and examining minutely the wealth of find-material; he even prefaced his book *On dating in the Bronze Age* (1885), which summarized these studies, with a sharp attack on Müller's arguments. The book reads like a manifesto for the typological method, and its presentation is so clear and well documented, that Scandinavian archaeology could now boast a leading figure. Though theoretical analysis of the method adopted by Montelius found Müller critical of the book, he was eventually obliged to admit that the results were right, and in 1909 he brought out a similar study of the Early Bronze Age which outdid Montelius in the detail of its chronology. Where the Swedish scholar had found three periods (with indications of earlier and later forms), Müller distinguished six.

These two approaches to the archaeological material, which we shall now briefly consider, naturally influenced one another to some extent but in the long run came to represent two different schools. Montelius gives the most thorough account of his method in the introduction to *Die älteren Kulturperioden im Orient und in Europa*, published in 1903. First he defined a number of generally accepted basic concepts whose content was not entirely clear.

'Relative chronology tells us whether an object is earlier or later than other objects. Absolute chronology tells us to which century before or after Christ the objects belong. To determine the relative chronology we must decide (1) which types are contemporaneous, i.e. belong to one and the same period, and (2) in what order the various periods occurred. It is not difficult to know which types are contemporaneous, once an adequate number of finds containing these types becomes available. None the less, in any typological investigation the state of the finds should always be studied with the utmost care.'

A find cannot be regarded as reliable unless it meets the following requirement: that all the objects when uncovered, were found under conditions clearly indicating that they were deposited together in the first place. When Montelius goes on to distinguish types and to order them in a series, he becomes more specific and his main concern seems to suggest ways of teaching the method rather than to define it exactly. In defining a type, emphasis is laid on the necessity of isolating distinctive features within each type. It is easy to see that this way of archaeological inquiry, which he had pioneered, was well adapted to an intuitive thinker like Montelius but more difficult for others to apply with the same lucidity. It was an equally difficult problem to order the types into an evolutionary sequence.

'I have given individual consideration to each of the main series of weapons, tools, ornaments, and pottery, together with their

79 Section of a tumulus near Dömmestorp, Scania, showing stratigraphy. A stone cist, more than two metres long, containing an uncremated body and bronze pin, occupies the central area. Above it, three cists containing cremated bones and bronze objects. Beside the uppermost cist is an urn. (After Montelius)

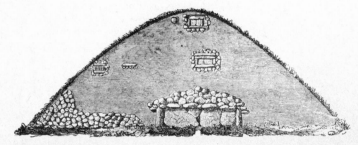

ornamentation, so as to determine the course of their evolution and to find out in what order the types – judged according to their own criteria – succeed each other.'

In reconstructing these sequences, Montelius worked from closed finds, stratigraphical data and the topography of burial-sites (a technique which went back to Vedel's discovery that the distribution of his 'cremation-pits' mirrored a chronological progression). Montelius was fully aware of the constant need for caution. For example, what appeared to be a closed find in a megalithic chamber might actually contain a more recent interment.

79

It was essential to start with as many finds as possible where different types occurred in association. Bronze Age burials were well suited to this sort of work, since they offered a wealth of comparative material and a relatively narrow range of types. The variants of each type could be arranged in series, and these series each underwent variations, though not necessarily in parallel. Certain types, like the fibulae, appeared to change at a more rapid pace than some of the other artifacts.

The differences between successive members of a typological series were very small, whereas the earliest and latest constituents would exhibit a comparatively large divergence. Thus a gradual process of change could be observed. Montelius took the simple functional form as a starting-point from which subsequent forms had developed. It seemed obvious that form had evolved from an earlier form of the series if it preserved vestiges of parts which had once been functional, just as in biological evolution. 'Parts of the object which formerly had a function have gradually lost their importance. Objects in which such features are still functional are necessarily older than objects where they are merely survivals.'

To check these typological series, Montelius used a method which he had already successfully put to the test in his monograph of 1885. To the type which he had placed earliest in the series he gave the letter A, to the next B, and so forth. He then introduced closed finds yielding exemplars from the various series into his schema. One result was the discovery that, for instance, fibulae of types A and B never occurred in a closed find containing hanging vessels. On the other hand, fibulae of type C were sometimes found with hanging vessels of type A. It followed that type A and B fibulae were older and that hanging vessels were not in use at that period. Then again, type F fibulae occurred in association with type B hanging vessels, and likewise, often, type G fibulae with type C and D hanging vessels; these groups would then be contemporaneous. This was also the case with type H fibulae and type E and F hanging vessels. On the other hand, type C fibulae did not appear in finds containing hanging vessels of types B–F, and type F fibulae were not found with hanging vessels of types A or C, D, E, F, etc. In this way associations of objects in finds could be used to establish parallel series which indicated contemporaneity, after the following pattern:

A – A
B – B
C – C

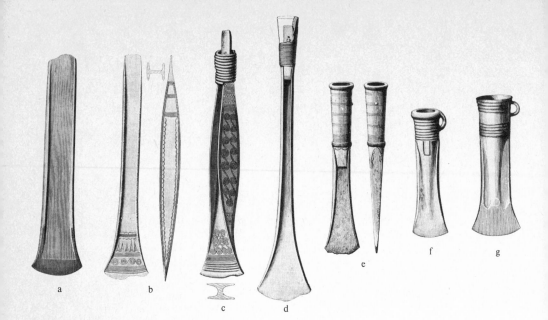

80 The development of the celt from the low flanged axe. In the case of (b), the original version (a) has been attached to an angled shaft and the edges progressively increase in height. In (c) a spiral has been introduced to hold the two prongs of the shaft together and prevent splitting. In (d) this spiral has fused with the axe. This feature is still evident in (e), where there are typological remnants of the spiral in the ornamentation. (f) With closely spaced horizontal grooves, and (g), with two sets of grooves, are regular celts with attached axe. (After Montelius, *Die Methode*))

80

where the parallelism was complete, or

A
   A
B
   B
C
D

which implied that types A and B of the first series were contemporaneous with type A of the second series.

It was another matter if a relationship like the following appeared between the series:

A
   B
B
C A
D E

Here there was no parallelism: either the typology was incorrect or else it was not applicable in that particular instance.

In the course of his discussion Montelius cited some specific examples of typological series, such as the celts. This tool – he postulated – had developed from the flat bronze axe on a curved shaft, the end of which was split so as to grip the thick end of the axe-blade. To prevent the wood from splitting further, the end of the shaft was fitted with a bronze spiral. The next phase was marked by a cast cylindrical shaft with grooves which imitated the original spiral, this ornamentation being a purely non-functional survival. Characterizing the subsequent stage was a heavy cast socket on the back of the blade, and last in the series comes a truncated version of the celt, with a socket running immediately above the blade and edge.

With his gift for teaching, Montelius illustrated this kind of development by showing how railway carriages had changed appearance over the years. The prototype consisted in essence, of stage-coaches combined into a single vehicle and mounted on flanged wheels. They retained, as a typological survival, their characteristic decorations along the sides. Gradually the carriage departed from this model and achieved a more functional design, but one feature which was long maintained was the outside entrance to each compartment.

Montelius' dating of the six Bronze Age periods was a particularly significant advance. To distinguish these periods, using typological criteria, called upon his entire extensive knowledge of European and Mediterranean chronology. He established that the oldest traces of bronze artifacts derived from the third millennium BC in Egypt. In Greece bronze was still in use in Mycenaean times, and iron was not adopted until *c.* 1000. In Italy, grave-finds from Bologna and Corneto testified to the use of iron in the ninth and eighth centuries. Since early Bronze Age artifacts found south and north of the Alps, such as triangular daggers, resembled each other closely in form, it could reasonably be assumed that the period began around the same date in both places, the mid-second millennium BC. The Iron Age apparently began in northern Europe in the fifth century or at the close of the sixth, since finds of imported Italian cylindrical bronze buckets appeared in association with the earliest Iron Age types in the north. These dates, then, marked the terminal limits of the Bronze Age; by further use of cross-dating, Montelius ascertained the duration and approximate dates of each of his sub-periods. These he tabulated against the phases of cultural development in northern Italy and the eastern part of central Europe.

The influence this book exerted on archaeological research has hardly a parallel among Scandinavian publications. In a single bold advance it brought this thousand-year-long period, previously so vaguely understood, into clear focus. The correctness of Montelius' main tenets on the Bronze Age was indisputable. The typological method itself, however, was arguable, even though he had applied it cautiously as a working hypothesis.

Montelius followed up his analysis of Bronze Age types in the

81

82

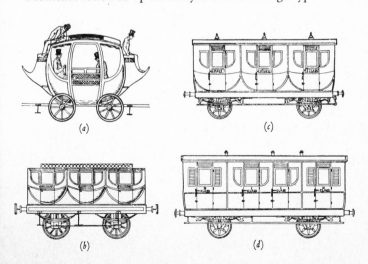

(a)

(b)

(c)

(d)

81 A typological series illustrated by Montelius: the development of the railway carriage from its prototype, the mail coach of *c.* 1825. In the second stage (*c.* 1840) the three carriages are simply made up of a series of coaches, as is evident from typological remnant-forms in the ornamentation. In the third stage (*c.* 1850) less dependence on the original is apparent, but there are still three side-entrances and an outside corridor. Even in the fourth stage the side-entrances are retained, though by now the ornamentation is largely independent of the prototype

early 1890s by using the same criteria to divide the later Stone Age into four periods and the Iron Age into eight; these results are still a fundamental part of the structure of modern archaeology. There was a logic behind even such features as the simple use of numbers to identify periods: it eliminated names which might misrepresent the true nature of the material. Illustrations of the main types of artifacts and a brief commentary on them were already for the most part provided by his *Swedish Antiquity* (*Sveriges forntid*), published in 1874 as a Swedish counterpart to Worsaae's volume of plates. It influenced the similar books which followed in Norway and Denmark, and was the basis for Montelius' last work, *Memories of our Antiquity* (*Minnen från vor forntid*), which came out in 1917.

Though attached to the State Historical Museum, Montelius enjoyed a position of virtual independence in Swedish antiquarian work. When the Svenska fornminnesförening was formed, in

82 The main artifact types of the Bronze Age, according to Montelius' system of 1881

1869, to counter the privileged status of the State Antiquary and the museum he directed, Montelius was considered a potential ally: in a few years he was the society's Secretary. His acuteness and unruffled diplomacy ensured that no antagonism arose between the expanding regional museums and the central state museum – an advantage to both sides, since there were ample opportunities for all concerned. In the widest sense, Montelius was a man who favoured order and harmony, and success did not desert him during his brief term as Royal Antiquary.

With the introduction of typology, the controversy over archaeological methods took on a new lease of life. Müller was its sternest critic, urging in *Aarboger* 1885 that classificatory and comparative techniques be used instead. He thought it permissible to identify constant types and to use these as a basis when classifying variants, but he opposed the idea of an evolution by law. To look for this kind of consistency, he stressed, was to forget the freedom of action, however limited by time and place, fixed rules and the tendency to imitate, which man enjoyed. His own method was

'simply to assemble as many points of comparison as possible. The first step in a comparative investigation is to consider every feature and component of the actual artifacts or other prehistoric material from a comparative point of view. Then, from the individual artifacts, this process is widened to take in the types, the complete finds, find-groups, and the entire available material – remembering all the time that nothing can be compared by and in itself, but only in its relation to other things: archaeological material, the condition of the find, and (most important) the find-spot. To use conclusions derived from pure analogy as a means of deducing the time and place of the material is bad method in all but rare cases; and it follows, moreover, that these conclusions as to affinity will not in themselves be binding unless the chronological and geographical relationships are known.'

The key word here is 'binding', which Müller applies to evidence which proves a genuine common background as opposed to a purely accidental resemblance.

He discussed the different varieties of similarity: first, a common origin, second, imitation, next, the sharing of more distant ancestors, whose descendants might be widely scattered in time and space, and, finally, a similarity of function or circumstances which may lead to the production of similar tools. He pointed out the usefulness of comparisons with the life-style and techniques of primitive peoples, which could in some cases be brought into the picture. The co-operation of latter-day craftsmen in experimenting with early tools was another means by which the comparative process could yield 'knowledge of prehistoric techniques in manufacture'. Signs of wear on the tools were an essential pre-condition, proving that the stone artifacts were in fact intended for specific use. In this connection, Müller also mentioned the help given by scientists – zoologists, chemists, botanists and others – in the interpretation of finds. This reasoning was admirable.

However, Müller did not accept certain parts of Montelius' system which was controlled by using closed finds. For the astonishing thing is that Montelius could order typological series

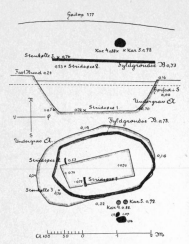

83 Single grave at Bindeballe, parish of Randbøl, central Jutland. *Top*: Section; *bottom*: plans of the interments: a lower grave (A) containing battle-axe 1; above it the floor-level grave (B), containing battle-axe 2; then an upper grave containing stone clubs and other objects. Above this again, interments from the Bronze and Iron Ages. (After S. Müller)

84 The second 'kitchen-midden commission', seven scholars who together investigated shell accumulations in Jutland and Zealand. From left to right, the geologist on the team, K.J.V. Steenstrup, the archaeologists A.P. Madsen (the artist), C. Neergaard, and Sophus Müller, who organized the project; the zoologists C.G.J. Petersen (a specialist in molluscs) and H. Winge (an osteologist); the botanist E. Rostrup. They are shown gathered around a remarkable find, the skeleton in the kitchen midden near Åmølle, Mariager fjord, east Jutland

and distinguish periods through intuition; his method presupposed a pattern of changing styles. And these stylistic phases ran a parallel course over large areas.

As we have seen, Müller eventually accepted Montelius' chronology of the Bronze Age, and added his own refinements to it. He had a sharp eye for details and an ability to shape the mass of disparate features into a meaningful synthesis, not only in the case of objective facts but also where the distribution of field-monuments through the countryside was concerned. He directed various investigations, but left the bulk of excavation work, together with the refinement of excavation technique, to members of his staff, who worked out a set of precise and effective rules. Subsequently, with help from various quarters, Müller was able to obtain government grants over a number of years to finance extensive excavations. In a paper published in *Aarbøger* (1897), covering the first few seasons, he took stock of the results with a justifiable feeling that he had used the available resources well. In his discussion of the Jutland single-grave culture in the same journal (1898) he made sophisticated use of the stratigraphical evidence, basing his chronological analysis of the culture on the three levels of interments, lower, ground and upper.

These are merely some of the remarkable results obtained during this intensive period of excavation. Müller was instrumental in forming a second commission of archaeologists and scientists to re-examine the chronology of the kitchen-middens, still a controversial question. After a series of careful excavations, published 1900 in a monograph, they arrived at the conclusion that the period of the kitchen-middens, the Early Stone Age, could be clearly distinguished – in spite of transitional phases – from a later, Neolithic period. Not long after, however, an even earlier phase of the Stone Age was recognized – thanks to an amateur's initial observations – at Maglemose (Zealand) by G. Sarauw, a member of the staff of the National Museum with a training in the natural sciences; his findings were published in *Aarbøger* (1903). Another investigation which deserves mention is the survey and interpretation of Danevirke and Kovirke, carried out by a team of archaeologists under Müller's leadership; his supposition in the publication of 1903 that the semicircular wall originally defended a town was later confirmed by excavations. In spite of being a genuine Copenhagener, Müller enjoyed the open air and the countryside; he studied the characteristic ways in which field-monuments were sited and made the acute observation in 1904 that barrows disposed in long lines or in concentrations marked, respectively, old pathways and settlements.

Like Worsaae and Montelius, Müller produced an illustrated manual, *Ordning af Danmarks Oldsager*, 1888–95, in which the different types of artifacts were lucidly ordered. Outstanding new finds such as the Trundholm sun-chariot, the Gundestrup cauldron, and the Juellinge burials were accorded detailed publications, and their broader implications well explored. He knew, moreover, how to communicate enthusiasm when describing his subject to

85 Excavation of the kitchen midden at Ertebølle. The work is being efficiently carried out by old people from the village, supervised by the archaeologists

86 A long line of barrows in Havredal south of Viborg, indicates the alignment of an ancient road. (After S. Müller)

 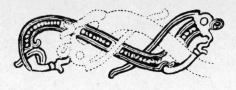

87 Zoomorphic ornamentation identified by Sophus Müller (*Aarbøger* 1881). *Left*: Migration style; *right*: Viking style

a lay audience; few introductory books can match *Vor Oldtid* for vigour and pertinacity of presentation. His description of the National Museum on the hundredth anniversary of its founding shows how wide was his knowledge of its traditions and collections. The style, though often involved, is clear, at times pointed and epigrammatic; but above all it conveys a sense of personal involvement which carries the reader along.

His work on prehistoric artifacts, many of them finely decorated, was informed by a warm feeling for art. Logically enough, his doctoral thesis was devoted to zoomorphic ornamentation. In this pioneering discussion, published in *Aarbøger*, 1880, he analysed both animal motifs of the Migration period and the distinctive styles of the Viking Age. Ornamentation was the theme also of his last books, on the art of the Stone, Bronze and Early Iron Ages. Indeed, he considered these publications to cover the finest achievements of prehistoric man.

87

Like Montelius, Müller ranged far beyond the limits of his own country in his studies, establishing a series of contacts and antecedents which extended as far as the Orient. It was here that both of them looked for the background of European development. Between them they exerted immense influence on the interpretation of prehistory; their ideas were developed further at the hands of such scholars as Gordon Childe, who was led by new excavations to emphasize afresh the important early cultural advances in the Middle and Near East.

Chapter Seven

Recent Norwegian Archaeology

THE ideas developed by Montelius and Müller were taken up and discussed throughout Scandinavia. There were differences of opinion, as in the case of H. Shetelig in Bergen and A. W. Brøgger in Oslo, two highly gifted Norwegian scholars who achieved prominence in the years after 1900. Within Norway, they acquired a standing comparable with that of Müller in Denmark and Montelius in Sweden; even though they did not see eye to eye, they worked in close collaboration, and Norwegian archaeology benefited greatly from this spirit of co-operation.

Also engaged in archaeology were a number of other productive scholars working in the country's five archaeological institutions, the regional museums. These museums enjoyed equal status and were together responsible for antiquarian work throughout Norway. Oslo and Bergen each had one, the others being in Stavanger, Trondheim and Tromsø.

We ought, however, to begin with the generation contemporary with Montelius and Müller, represented first and foremost by Oluf Rygh and Ingvald Undset. Rygh succeeded Keyser as Professor of History and Director of the University Archaeological Museum in 1862, after being associated with it for two years. Realizing that he could not combine the disciplines of Archaeology and History, he had a Chair established in Scandinavian Archaeology in 1875, to which he himself was appointed. Meanwhile, he had devoted much time and energy to an important project, the compilation of Norwegian farm names. He is best known for his book on Late Iron Age Norway (1877) and for *Norwegian Antiquities* (*Norske Oldsager*) (1880–5), a counterpart to the general surveys of types produced by Müller and Montelius. This is a substantial, well-annotated work. He possessed a thorough knowledge of the material, having catalogued some twenty thousand artifacts between 1861 and 1899.[72]

88 O. Rygh (1833–99)

Undset, his assistant from 1875 onwards, was a scholar of a different type. He was able to spend the greater part of his time in independent study, travelling frequently, was well acquainted with European museums and a familiar figure at international congresses.[73] Being in the enviable position of drawing an emolument direct from the Treasury, he was sought after as a supernumerary professor. He was regarded as a scholar of great promise, but he died prematurely at the age of forty. Undset produced one major work, *The Beginning of the Iron Age in Northern Europe* (*Jernalderens Begyndelse i Nord-Europa*), published in 1881. In his

89 I. Undset (1853–93)

research he was influenced by Montelius, whom he first met when twenty-one years old, at the international congress of archaeologists of 1874 in Stockholm; this meeting with Montelius, ten years his senior, crystallized his aims and the methods he was to adopt. The object of his monograph was to distinguish the dominant culture areas, with which his travels had made him familiar. He started with Early Iron Age Italy, tracing this culture up into the Alps and central Europe, proceeding thence to a detailed examination of the northern European finds, whose earliest phase he was able to place in the context of the southern groups; he was also able to prove the existence of a pre-Roman Iron Age in Norway.

Undset's work attracted wide attention, especially with the appearance of a German translation the following year. His comments and illustrations have continued to be of value, in part because objects he examined have since disappeared. Unlike Rygh and Montelius, it was not his aim to produce a systematic ordering of the types. On the other hand, he was a lively writer, with a sensitivity for art, and in his memoirs *Fra Akershus til Akropolis* (1892) he gives a fascinating description of his travels and of fellow-archaeologists from many countries. He shows special perceptiveness in describing Denmark, with which he had strong ties of sympathy.

Rygh, the diligent systematist, 'felt no love for the finds as such and was displeased by the general excitement over the Gokstad ship, because it represented from his specialist viewpoint merely a number in a catalogue like a flint arrowhead or an iron axe';[74] whereas Undset was a man of intuition, with enthusiasm for his material and the ability to communicate this pleasure in books and articles for newspapers and learned journals, thereby creating a popular following.

Active in archaeology, but without the same background of training as Rygh and Undset, were Nicolaysen and Lorange. Nicolaysen's reputation rested on his extensive experience of excavating burial-mounds, and also on his valuable topographical surveys. He was on the staff of the Society for preserving the Norwegian Monuments.[75] Anders Lorange was an archaeological assistant at the Bergen museum from 1873 until his death in 1888.[76] He showed more precision than his contemporaries in his approach to archaeological fieldwork, conducting a number of excavations in the south of Norway. His reports show his ability as an observer and his good fortune in discovering objects of exceptional value. Lorange's particular interest was the Iron Age – the swords of that period, for example – and after a reading of Vedel's first publication he pointed out that certain poor mound burials might antedate the Roman period, which he had discussed in a brief article 'On traces of Roman culture in Norway' (1875). It was Undset, however, who first provided conclusive evidence on the subject.

Rygh's successor was the Swede Gabriel Gustafson, who had developed an interest in prehistory and the excavations on Gotland, the home of his childhood years.[77] After studying at Uppsala, he joined the museum staff at Bergen. Thence he moved on to Oslo, where two major undertakings presented themselves:

overseeing the building for housing the University's archaeological collection (opened in 1904) and directing the excavation of the newly discovered Oseberg mound. Though Gustafson himself was not spared to publish the splendid grave-goods the latter was found to contain – among the richest of Scandinavian pre-history – he had previously brought some talented collaborators into the project and after his death in 1915 they completed the publication of his great work. Haakon Shetelig, Gustafson's successor as keeper in archaeology at Bergen, assisted ably in the investigation. The accompanying photographs give an impression of this ambitious excavation and the conditions under which it was carried out.

92 The Oseberg ship in the Viking Ship Hall on Bygdøy, Oslo

The conservation of the Oseberg ship, with its many finely carved wooden components, took several years, but publication and its installation in the Viking Ship Museum on Bygdøy, proved no less time-consuming a task. Here Gustafson's dynamic successor at Oslo, A. W. Brøgger, put in a lot of hard work. He raised money for the museum and persuaded the Storting to back publication of the material. In the monumental work, *Oseberg fundet*, that resulted can be found accounts of the ship and its construction, the art-work (by Shetelig), the royal quarters, as represented by its surviving furnishings (by S. Grieg), and a discussion of the many other questions posed by this unique monument. The buried woman's noble birth and her patronage of the arts made it possible to form a detailed impression of the highest stratum of Viking society and its most gifted artists. The world of the Viking imagination is, moreover, illustrated by the remarkable picture tapestry with its distinctive motifs, and the carved wagon with its mythical representations and strange art.

93 The third volume, dealing with the styles, contains a masterly account of the numerous wood-carvers, whose special aptitudes and characteristic traits are the subject of careful analysis. The influence of the typological method is evident in Shetelig's discussion here, since he groups his artists on a chronological basis, whereas other scholars might prefer to classify them and to regard them as representing an age when older and younger styles were simultaneously current. In his survey of this material, richly diverse and often of high quality, Shetelig forges a link between

the styles and their creators. He writes with the same classical lucidity as Montelius did in his work of 1885 on the Bronze Age.

Shetelig already had the benefit of a systematic grounding in archaeology from Rygh when, as a young man, he first arrived in Stockholm. There Montelius made him at home and introduced him to the methods of prehistoric archaeology.[78] This training and his methodical labours led him to write a doctoral thesis in 1907 on cruciform brooches in Norway. He described this group, relating it to the various other types of fibulae, their development and the parallels elsewhere. In the comparative section of his study he laid special emphasis on the English material, pointing to its continental antecedents.

As early as 1901 Shetelig became Director of the Department of Archaeology at the Bergen museum, spending the rest of his working life here (except for a few war-time years when he was removed from office). He was industrious as an excavator and expanded the museum to the point at which it became the logical nucleus for the new university. He attained professional standing in 1914, and as Director of the institution from 1938 he was a dominant figure in its scholarly life.

Besides being thoroughly familiar with Viking remains, Shetelig acquired a knowledge of their antecedents, examining and re-examining the numerous Iron Age burial finds from the west of Norway. He adopted the same attitude toward the region's Stone Age dwelling-sites, in order to extract from them as much information as possible. He suggested how the Nydam boat and other ship finds could be regarded as forerunners of the Viking ships, on which he produced a book in collaboration with Brøgger. In order to compile and publish the evidence for Scandinavian contacts with western Europe, particularly Britain and Ireland, he enlisted the co-operation of his Norwegian colleagues shortly before the war; therefore, this compilation of the archaeological material never progressed beyond a preliminary stage. Nevertheless, with the subsequent presentation of his general conclusions under the title *Viking Antiquities*, Shetelig can be credited with a fine, well-argued essay in cultural history. Certain aspects of this material he had already discussed long before, such as the remarkable stone crosses on the Isle of Man – first observed by Worsaae – which he now brought into precise correlation with Scandinavian styles.

The penetration and insight that characterized Shetelig's studies can be gauged from both his short book on prehistoric Norway and one on Scandinavian prehistory (written in collaboration with H. Falk). His essays show an instinct for the telling details that bring prehistory to life.

Brøgger was a different but no less important figure.[79] To him prehistory meant chiefly cultural history, and he studied the source material from this point of view, trying to find answers to new types of questions. Because of this new approach to the finds, the attempt to set them in a wider context, he was criticized from time to time and himself experienced occasional lapses in confidence, but his effect was stimulating, like a breath of fresh air through the schemas of Scandinavian archaeology. In his book, *The Norwegian*

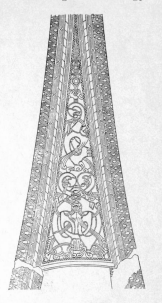

93 Detail of the ornament on a sledge-pole, executed by 'the Academician', as Shetelig characterized the painstaking woodcarver who was responsible for a number of Oseberg objects. (After Shetelig)

94 A.W. Brøgger (1884–1951)

People in Prehistory (*Det norske Folk i Oldtiden*), he broke with many scholarly conventions. He placed less importance on the three-age system, taking it for what it was, a model based on the changing materials, and instead emphasized the functional aspects of the finds – hunting culture, agriculture and husbandry, Celtic influence on Iron Age tools, the interplay between the means of sustenance and the natural environment, and so on. He studied the material for its social implications. This is not to say that he dispensed with detailed investigations – he had several to his credit – but rather that he regarded prehistory, back to its remotest beginnings, as a direct forerunner of the present and made it his aim to show this was so.

A lasting influence on Brøgger was his early collaboration with his father, the prominent geologist W. C. Brøgger, in studies of the coastline; by degrees, however, the son's interests came to centre on the archaeological side of the investigations, the Stone Age finds and their significance as a means of dating the changing sea levels. He persisted on his own in this pursuit, using his coastline observations in his study of the Nøstvet axe (1905), the first proper analysis of the Early Stone Age in Norway.

A further contribution to the understanding of Early Stone Age culture came with his doctoral thesis, *The Arctic Stone Age in Norway* (*Den arktiske stenalder i Norge*), a wide-ranging comparative study which drew on newly discovered finds.

After this period of independent study, Brøgger joined the staff of the Stavanger museum, becoming Deputy Director of the University archaeological collection in Oslo in 1913 and two years later professor and director. He found ample scope there for his talents as an administrator. The part he played, through tenacity and charm, in ensuring that the Oseberg find was fittingly exhibited and published has already been mentioned. *Norske Oldfund*, a monograph series, was begun around the same time, and in 1917 he founded the periodical *Oldtiden*. From 1899 the Society for preserving Norwegian Monuments concentrated on remains from the medieval and later periods, but thanks to Brøgger conferences of archaeologists from the five museums responsible for prehistoric monuments took place, becoming a regular institution from 1927 onward. He must also be given credit for the steps he took to protect areas of exceptional prehistoric interest, like Borre, and, generally, to improve the position of archaeology, not least by expanding his own staff and strengthening the conservation department.

For his own research he selected topics which had previously been overlooked, such as the old system of weights. This he reconstructed in part from finds of Late Iron Age weights and in part by calculating the unit of weight whereby gold rings and other valuables from the period were assessed. His book on this complex question, *Ertog og Øre*, showed what possibilities lay in the field of prehistory.

In this particular brand of research he made full use of both historical and archaeological sources. An instance is his *Ancient Emigrants*, where he tackles the problem of finding a date for the westward emigration of the Scandinavians. Rightly, he laid considerable stress on finds from the islands off Scotland and even though some of his datings have since proved untenable the book is a valuable work of synthesis, discussing as it does the finds in the light of evidence from written sources. He adopted the same approach in his lively account of the battle of Stiklastaoir (1030), dealing with the weaponry then in use, the battlefield, the invasion route from the east, and the descriptions of this celebrated event which have come down to us.

Brøgger's contribution was a very personal and also a very fertile one: 1936 saw the founding of the Norwegian Archaeological Society and of the journal *Viking*; in the same year, when he was president of the international congress of archaeologists, Brøgger's Viking Museum on Bygdøy was deservedly a centre of attraction. He was proud to introduce this large assembly of archaeologists to his country's splendid scenery and prehistoric monuments. The vigorous personality of the man, involved as he was in administration, writing and politics, commanded general respect. He was a prominent figure in the University, stoutly defending its independent position during the Nazi occupation, as a result of which he and his closest colleagues were imprisoned. After his release, however, he devoted his last years to the archaeological collection and to his profession.

At the Stavanger museum Brøgger was followed by Jan Petersen, whose brother was head of the Trondheim museum. Petersen is best remembered for three valuable publications, dealing with the weapons, ornaments and tools of the Viking Age. In his work, too, the influence of Montelius can be detected; his *Norwegian Viking Swords*, published in 1919, is sub-titled 'a typological-chronological study'. His first step was to establish the limits of the period, classifying as earliest the types which agreed with those of the previous period and as latest those which occurred in medieval finds. Between these extremes he ordered his series of swords, shield-bosses, spearheads, etc., verifying the typological series from the large body of closed finds, just as Montelius had done. Except for rich burials like Gjermundbu, the subject of a detailed report by S. Grieg, and the Viking ship burials, the actual finds have not yet been published in full.

95 Jan Petersen (1887–1967)

Both Petersen and the Deputy Director of the archaeological collection, Helge Gjessing, who met an untimely death, conducted systematic excavations of Iron Age house-sites in southern Norway, working under difficult conditions. Their aim was to gain information on house-construction and agricultural practices, a project which had Brøgger's whole-hearted support.

A lively spirit of independence characterized the generation of archaeologists who were active during the first half of this century, and it influenced the way archaeological work continued in Norway. Legislation was approved on 13 July 1905, soon after Norway attained nationhood, to protect all prehistoric monuments and to entitle the State to all finds. It was the finder's duty to surrender his finds, and in certain cases he would be recompensed. And since, thanks to the centuries of dependence, Norway had never developed an administrative capital of her own, it was possible to decentralize the conservation authority – a desideratum because of the vast area to be covered – and to confer equal responsibility on each of the five principal museums. These, as has already been mentioned, were at Oslo, Stavanger, Bergen, Trondheim and Tromsø; only one of them was in fact a State institution, but, typically, this was considered no obstacle to their taking on antiquarian duties, though one more has since been accorded that status. The essential point, however, is that the five museums were placed on an equal footing and that endeavours were made to engage professional staff, who could make the work of the museum their full-time occupation, an objective that was gradually realized. The same principle of equality applied to museums which functioned as part of a university: although the staff at Bergen and Oslo had teaching responsibilities, the museum as such acquired no additional standing, beyond the need to employ more people. A separation between museum work and antiquarian duties, as found in such countries as Sweden, did not develop in Norway. A Riksantikvariat was set up in Oslo, but its province was the medieval period and later.

The two most recent museums, that at Tromsø which was founded in 1872 and included Nicolaysen's collections, and that at Stavanger which was founded in 1877, with a department of cultural history since 1909, were strengthened in the same way as the others, and with the increased activity in excavation they came by degrees into their own.

In Norway, then, the history of antiquarian institutions took a special course, a result of such factors as the geography of the country and the need to delegate duties to regional institutions which were in closer touch with work in the field than a national administration.

Chapter Eight

Recent Swedish Archaeology

ON his retirement Montelius could look back on an impressive series of contributions to archaeological science. Moreover, his diplomacy had restored good relations between the National Antiquarian Institution in Stockholm, the expanding regional museums, and the universities. The last-named had plans to begin teaching prehistoric archaeology, which necessitated access to good collections.

But this was not the only problem. The State Historical Museum occupied such cramped accommodation in the Gothic-vaulted   96
basement of the National Museum that the need for new quarters was imperative. In addition, if the law protecting monuments was to work, all prehistoric remains in the country had to be recorded, a process of reconnaissance and scheduling which in Denmark had continued for several decades after Worsaae first started the project. In 1942 the law was extended to cover, among other things, the natural environs of the monuments. What is more, already scheduled monuments had to be inspected and newly discovered finds excavated, two tasks which were entrusted in the 1930s to district antiquaries appointed partly on a State, partly on a local basis. Each of these district antiquaries took charge of a large local museum and directed antiquarian work within his own region, of which there were upwards of twenty in all. It was to be expected that these hard-worked officials, quite a number of whom were professional archaeologists, would find it necessary to employ specialist staff. Those without experience in archaeological field-work accordingly took on prehistorians as assistants.

This elaborate structure was presided over by the Royal Antiquary, who had also to direct the State Historical Museum; on the other hand, the museum and the antiquarian administration each had its own separate staff of research-workers and assistants. This process of change began in earnest during S. Curman's term as Royal Antiquary. Showing energy and vision, he inaugurated a nation-wide survey; and although the number of field-monuments alone must be in excess of half a million, the project is now complete over some parts of the country. Concurrently, aerial photography is being used in the preparation of new national survey maps, on which prehistoric remains are to be shown with special symbols. The Riksantikvariat took charge of all this work, together with the organization of rescue digs.

Curman, who specialized in the Middle Ages and architectural history, showed equal tenacity in finding better accommodation

96 for the museum. He acquired a large building and had it converted
to provide modern facilities for exhibition and storage, for housing the extensive archives, as well as office space for the Royal
Antiquary's administration and the State Historical Museum.
Though in this way antiquarian work continued to be centralized
in Stockholm, important aspects of it were delegated to the district
antiquaries, while the universities were given more scope for
action. The central institution continued to hold responsibility
where legal and political questions were concerned. At the same
time the university institutions were gradually being strengthened
and – a lengthy process – brought into conformity with the
97 official State organization. The museums at Lund and Uppsala
both had long histories, the one at Lund being – as we have seen –
among the oldest collections in Scandinavia. At Uppsala the
establishment of a rune-stone museum was discussed by the
University in 1725, and a few years later the plan was carried out.[80]
With the approval of the Royal Antiquary (but without permission
from the Chancellery) three stones were exhibited. Though it
possessed a few other prehistoric artifacts, which were displayed
in a case of *objets d'art*, the museum became a reality only with the
benefaction of J. H. Schröder, the man to whom Thomsen first
expounded his three-age system. The collection, housed in the
Gustavianum, was enlarged further through donations and purchases, but its primary emphasis continued to be on stone objects.

In 1872 the museum was moved to the County hospital and
subsequently to an orangery in the botanical gardens which

96 The State Historical Museum,
Stockholm. *Top*: The Stone Age
exhibition when it was in the
basement of the National
Museum, 1904; *bottom*: the
modern exhibition of Viking
period finds in its new
surroundings

97 The University Museum of
Scandinavian Antiquities,
Uppsala (before 1921)

98 O. Almgren (1869–1945)

Rudbeck had once laid out. Here the exhibition cases were flanked
by Fogelberg's classical statues of Odin and Balder; prehistoric
remains were confronted by manifestations of Romantic and
Gothic taste. However, there were certain restrictions there, and
in 1921 the museum was re-installed in the Gustavianum, its
natural home, where the Antikvitetscollegium had flourished and
Rudbeck had been a regular visitor.

New life entered into the institution with the creation of a
Department of Scandinavian Prehistory, first directed by K.
Stjerna. His brief time there, 1905 to 1909, gave rise to some
excavation work, and his successor, O. Almgren, appointed to a
Chair in 1914, gained standing as a scholar and by virtue of his
field and excavation work. But the museum really came into its
own under S. Lindqvist, the man who was responsible, together
with his assistants, for recovering such rich finds from the Valsgärde burial-ground. By recognizing the special standing of the
museum in 1952 and permitting it to keep these important new
finds the Royal Antiquary showed a flexible attitude.

The Historical Museum of Lund University had old and deep
roots. The Skåne countryside was fertile in finds, and the University enjoyed an unquestioned right to retain them, having
recovered quite a number through its own excavations. Until
1904 the collection was supervised by a history professor, but then
O. Rydbeck, who had been a lecturer for a couple of years and
had just taken his doctorate, was appointed Director. From then
on its growth was rapid. It was moved from the cellar underneath
the Great Hall of the University to better accommodation on the
ground floor of the Lundagård. Later, with Rydbeck's copious
acquisitions, some of them medieval finds, a second removal, to
the present building opposite the cathedral, became imperative.
It developed naturally into the principal museum and research
institution in the south of Sweden. In 1919 the post was upgraded
to a professorship in prehistoric and medieval archaeology.
Rydbeck's interest in both these subjects played its part in deter-
mining the responsibilities of the post.

The University of Stockholm had of course only to turn to the
State Historical Museum for a comprehensive study collection,
and some years later, under N. Åberg, the third to occupy a Chair
in Archaeology, an official course of study was set up. Finally, the

99 O. Rydbeck (1872–1954)

100 N. Åberg (1888–1957)

significant archaeological museum at Göteborg functioned directly as a university museum for a time, though the Chair now established there has no connection with the work of the museum.

The position, then, in Sweden is that, aside from the national antiquarian administration – the office of the Royal Antiquary and the State Historical Museum – there exist two university museums under professorial directorship, both the outcome of special historical factors; two more recent university institutions without museum duties; and finally a great number of local archaeological museums. Of these, the collection at Visby is among the oldest and most important, with Gotland, in prehistoric times a wealthy trading centre, as its catchment area.

Such a wide range of activity, but in particular the increased opportunities for research which came, for example, with the State foundation for the humanities, had its effect on archaeology. Even so, the two generations which followed Montelius saw only gradual progress and expansion. Many new periodicals and monograph series came into being, publications which are still being produced – one thinks of *Fornvännen* (Stockholm), *Tor* (Uppsala), and the monograph series of the Vitterhetsakademi and the Universities of Lund and Uppsala.

In *Die Altgermanische Thierornamentik* (1904) Montelius' successor, Bernhard Salin, made a penetrating analysis of the types of zoomorphic ornamentation dating from the fifth to the eighth century, and his book is still a standard text for students of style. Artistically gifted, he had a keen eye for details and combinations, accurately discerning the constituent motifs, however cunningly concealed within the maze of interlace work. He distinguished three styles: I, the counterpart of Müller's Migration style; II, that depicting animals with interlaced ribbon bodies, best represented by rich burial finds from Vendel in Uppland; and III, that which took in sophisticated later forms. The characteristic motifs of each group, such as animal heads, limbs and bodies, were analysed, and acutely characterized. Illness prematurely prevented Salin, a scholar of considerable gifts, from continuing his research and professional work.

101 B. Salin (1861–1931)

An equally fundamental book is Almgren's *Studien über nordeuropäische Fibelformen der ersten nachchristlichen Jahrhunderte* (1897), which immediately won its author wide recognition. With a keen eye for the possible ways of grouping the fibulae, Almgren divided the material into seven principal categories, which have since been accepted as essentially correct. Part of the ground-work was no doubt already provided by Hildebrand's studies of 1872, but Almgren's painstaking museum study enabled him not only to add considerably to the material, but to order it on typological principles. Following Montelius' lead, he used closed finds as a means of verifying his results and showed that the types indicated a division into early and late phases in both Montelius' period IV and V (the Early and Late Roman Iron Age respectively). The book became a standard work and has served its purpose, though the

102 Salin's styles I–III

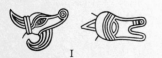 

I   II   III

evidence on which it was based has naturally been affected to some extent by new finds and observations. The essential thing was that the brooches were placed in the wider context to which they belonged; one aspect was treated in a brief but important paper (1913) on the significant role the Marcomannic kingdom played in developing the earliest Roman Iron Age types.

His *Rock Engravings and Cult (Hällristninger och kultbruk)* shows Almgren's ability to correlate manifestations relating to religious customs. These remarkable pictures, carved on rocks, were already known to Renaissance antiquaries, and around the turn of the present century Baltzer had brought out picture-books showing the richly decorated rock faces of Bohuslän. Almgren now addressed himself to a systematic investigation of the meaning behind these motifs, using folklore and bringing in parallels from a wide variety of sources. The book that resulted was a stimulating essay in the interpretation of a primitive, long-forgotten mode of thought. While studying archaeological material, he noticed a special pattern of cultural development in Gotland, conducted excavations at a number of burial-sites, and in 1914 published the first volume of his typological analysis, which included an account of Early Iron Age Gotland. At a comparatively early age, however, Almgren's sight began to fail, restricting his activities. The second volume, on the period AD 200–400, was published in 1923 in collaboration with B. Nerman, who for some years was Director of the State Historical Museum, and it was Nerman who continued the series, with a special discussion of burial finds from Gotland dating from between 550 and 800. He traced the course of Late Iron Age Swedish expansion over a variety of regions, among them Latvia, where he investigated the cemeteries and fortifications at Grobin, a settlement of colonists from Gotland and eastern Sweden which flourished during the centuries immediately prior to the Viking Age.

The Baltic region became a focus of much intensive study, particularly after the publication in 1905 of K. Stjerna's thoughtful monograph, *The Population development of Bornholm in the Iron Age (Bidrag till Bornholms befolkningshistoria under järnålderen)*. Here he takes into account finds from Gotland and Öland as well as the Bornholm material. Treating these islands as an entity, he pointed out unmistakable evidence of contact between them and went so far as to suggest an emigration from Bornholm as the cause of a hiatus in the find-material around AD 550. In its typological analysis the book shows the influence of Montelius and notwithstanding some rather sweeping statements the author's talent and his profound knowledge of the material are clearly evident from its pages. Although Stjerna's theories do not tally with the observations of Vedel and have been criticized by Danish scholars, this does not detract from the importance of his work. A great loss was suffered with his early death.

Almgren's successor, S. Lindqvist, continued research into some of the topics which Stjerna had taken up, concentrating especially in his large output on the rich Vendel burial-ground and the evidence it provided of foreign contacts (*Vendelkulturens ålder och ursprung*, 1926). He is especially remembered for his investigation

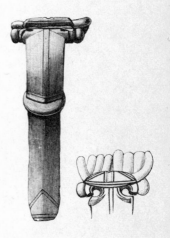

103 Fibula types as illustrated in Almgren's *Fibelformen*. Examples from groups II, III and IV

104 Viking-style sword-pommel with openwork, found in Russia (Gnezdovo). In Scandinavia this use of openwork is characteristic of oval fibulae but not of swords

of the outstanding Valsgärde cemetery, where boat-burials were found which closely resembled those at Vendel and yielded important additional information. Lindqvist, with his intuitive feeling for style, was well equipped to write up these finds himself, but he preferred to leave the task of publication to his two closest associates, G. Arwidson and P. Olsen, whose stylistic analyses form a major addition to Salin's system. Lindqvist himself published two important find-groups, the large, famous Late Iron Age tumuli of Uppland and the picture-stones of Gotland, which he ordered and presented in a form convenient for subsequent research. In his numerous short surveys and special studies his originality and stimulating talent are constantly in evidence.

Vendel had been painstakingly excavated by H. Stolpe and publication was completed as early as 1912 at the hands of T.J. Arne, the distinguished Director of the Iron Age Department of the State Historical Museum. Later, in 1934, he published another related site of great importance, namely Tune (Alsike), and discussed the connection between finds made there and those of other burials from the same period. Arne, however, is best remembered for his authoritative work on Scandinavian Viking Age finds in Russia, together with their analogues in Scandinavia. In his doctoral thesis (1914), 'La Suède et l'Orient', he laboriously assembled this widely dispersed material, describing and analysing it. Comparing Russian with Scandinavian types, he found that while some were identical, others, found in Russia, showed certain combinations of stylistic features which did not occur in Scandinavia. Collectively, he explained the finds in the light of historical sources as resulting from the eastward expansion of the Swedes, a line of reasoning which has since led to lively argument.

While Arne, who followed up his studies of eastern cultures with a series of expeditions, was working toward a solution of Iron Age problems, some of his colleagues at the State Historical Museum were engaged in investigations of the Stone and Bronze Ages. O. Frödin carried out some interesting excavations of neolithic settlements in an area of swamps at Alvastra. Other aspects of the Late Stone Age were studied by A. Bagge, who produced a series of monographs on megalithic grave-finds (in collaboration with L. Kaelas). Important, too, is the investigation into the Siretorp settlement in Blekinge, to which he (and Kjellmark) devoted a detailed publication. A clear stratigraphy could be made out, with three separate layers, the upper and lower being neolithic and the middle one attesting a fishing settlement. Here was clear evidence that a fishing culture continued to exist side by side with a farming culture. He attributed the special culture found in Late Stone Age settlements in the east and south of Sweden to contacts with the east.

A valuable feature of A. Oldeberg's work on the Bronze Age, which he prefaces with a discussion of the fibulae, is the co-operation he received from metallurgists, which made possible an understanding of production techniques. He enlisted their collaboration again later in a study of Viking Age metalwork.

As early as 1928, the theory of a tradition extending down from the fishing culture of the Early Stone Age to a period when agri-

105

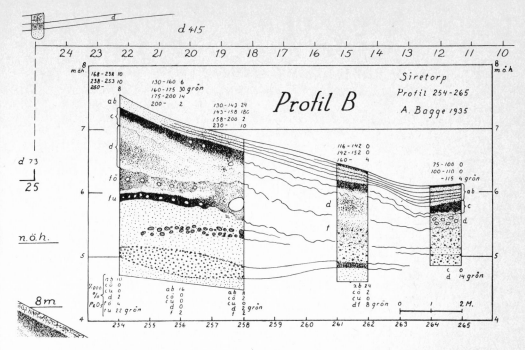

culture had become widely practised was put forward by Rydbeck in his paper on *The Levels of the Stone Age Sea and the Oldest Inhabitants of Scandinavia* (*Stenåldershavets nivaaförändringar och Nordens äldsta bebyggelse*). At the time it caused a sensation, and it was only by degrees, partly through finds in Denmark, that the theory won acceptance. Ten years later, Rydbeck reopened the question, touching on such points as the tradition of fishing culture during the Stone Age in southern Scandinavia, which also provoked lively debate. He was whole-heartedly supported in all this by his gifted pupil, J. E. Forssander, who succeeded him in the Chair but was to die young. During his academic career Forssander devoted himself to solving certain major problems in this field. He developed a highly individual mode of presentation, suited to his eloquent exposition of interpretations. In the time that intervened between his thesis (1933) on the Swedish boat-axe culture and a paper of 1943, seeking to establish Irish influence on Scandinavian ornamentation in the early Viking Age, he wrote extensively, touching on every aspect of Scandinavian prehistory. Apparent in the best of these works, such as *East Scandinavia in the oldest metal period of Europe* (*Ostskandinavien i Europas äldsta metaltid*, 1936) and *Provinzialrömisches und Germanisches* (1937), are acute gifts of observation and an ability to marshal convincing arguments. He divided the early metal culture of Europe, the Copper and Bronze Age, into phases and discussed the various geographical foci in the evolution of this culture. He underlined the importance of the central Danube area for the early stages, later to be superseded by the central Danube European Unětice culture and Insular developments. The first bronze-casting in Scandinavia appears midway through the stone cist period, under Insular influence. Over the next phase the influence of the tumulus-burial region in central Europe can be recognized. As can be seen, Forssander worked on

105 Stratigraphy at Siretorp, Blekinge. Layer ab contains pit-decorated ceramics; layer c, corded ware. (After Bagge)

106 J. E. Forssander (1904–44)

107 (a) Sösdala and (b) Sjörup styles of decoration; two examples from bog finds in Scania (fifth and sixth centuries AD)

the basis of Montelius' and Müller's theories but provided a more differentiated background.

In another, equally important, paper, dealing with two Skåne hoards dating from the fifth or sixth century, Forssander showed how Style I, the characteristic mode of ornamentation in the metal mountings uncovered in Sjörup, had a forerunner dating from around AD 400, with embossed decoration and more simply formed animal motifs. This earlier style occurs in the other Skåne find, at Sösdala. Like Style I, it has antecedents in Europe, though its special characteristics were acquired in Scandinavia.

Forssander's studies of certain aspects of the Neolithic period are of particular interest; he addressed himself in the first place to excavations of megalithic graves, which he related to a contemporary type of settlement peculiar to the south of Sweden. Whereas O. Lidén, who published a number of settlement finds, considered them to be a local development, Forssander took them to represent an integral part of the peasant culture of the megalithic burial period.

Just as determined in his selection of topics but quite different in his approach was N. Åberg, who was familiar with the entire prehistory of Europe. A large part of his comprehensive, lucidly written output is available in the principal world languages; he is best remembered for his impressive series of studies in Bronze and Early Iron Age chronology. These, like his books in general, provide a convenient and sound introduction to the European background of Scandinavian culture. Few other scholars could rival his first-hand knowledge of the find-material and its potentialities.

A pupil of Montelius, Åberg developed a clear understanding of the nature of typology and described the method in accordance with his own use of it; in this form it found wide application in Scandinavian prehistory. True typology, in his view, entailed an insight akin to the artist's into a given body of material; by the exercise of intuition it was possible to group this material into early and late forms. Although, as we have seen, Åberg concentrated on certain chronological and typological problems, he recognized that in reality they were expressions of culture-historical phenomena, and from this angle in the closing years of his career he studied the historical relationship between the later Roman period, the Migration era and the Vendel period (to use the Swedish term), treating different forms of contact, through trade or war, and the rise of cultural and political centres.

108 H. Arbman (1904–68)

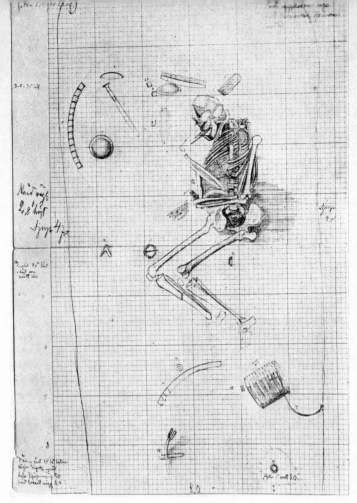

109 A grave at Birka, drawn by
H. Stolpe and published by
Arbman

The same enthusiasm for Scandinavian prehistory and its contacts with the south, east and west was demonstrated by H.   108
Arbman, who was for many years at the State Historical Museum
and then from 1945 until his death in 1968 occupied the Chair at
Lund. He was a keen observer, an engaging writer, widely
travelled, and carried out many excavations. He dug a number of
times, for example, in Normandy, in search of evidence of the
Scandinavian occupation.

At an early stage of his career he began working within the
special field which became his chief interest. In 1931 he was
entrusted with the task of publishing the rich burials from the
Viking town of Birka. As mentioned, H. Stolpe had carried the   109
excavation itself through in a capable manner, but did not publish
his findings. Arbman presented the material in two handy volumes
(1940 and 1943), reserving the synthesis and conclusions for later
publication. He had already tackled some major problems in his
dissertation (1937) on Sweden and the Frankish kingdom, also
taking into account the relations with other culture areas. Rightly,
he stressed the significance of such imports as glass and pottery,
which, like acanthus ornamentation and other artistic impulses,
originated with the great west-European kingdom. He returned
to the problems of the Viking Age on several occasions, among

104 other things making a thorough re-appraisal of Scandinavian contacts with Russia. He studied ornaments and weapons, among them some finds from central Russia, and showed that their ornamentation represented a blend of Russian and Scandinavian styles. He was led by this evidence to support Arne's theory of a Viking civilization in Russia, exploring the implications of the idea in a short book, *Svear i Österviking*. In another, equally readable introductory work, written in collaboration with M. Stenberger, he described the Viking expeditions to the west; he produced works for both the scholarly and the general reader on Birka and the Viking period as a whole.

Arbman's attention turned, naturally enough, to a consideration of similar types of problems which cropped up in connection with the centuries prior to the Viking period. He was interested primarily in the development of art over these centuries. This work led to such noteworthy results as his demonstration of contact between eastern Scandinavia and the central Danube area in the sixth century and his discussion of the Childeric find and the complex of stone-lined cells, all accompanied with significant observations which have an important bearing on Scandinavian prehistory as well. He touched on the Roman Iron Age in his excavation, later published, of the bog-find in Käringsjön, and produced evidence on the beginning of the Iron.Age in the shape of a significant, though often not outwardly impressive, assemblage of finds.

Stenberger, a contemporary of Arbman's, who went on industriously producing new work until his death early in 1973, was a scholar of predominantly Scandinavian interests whose career well illustrates the opportunities for research available in Sweden. Beginning as curator of the Gotland museum, with all its scope for excavation work, he went on to the Iron Age Department of the State Historical Museum, and from there to occupy the Chair at Uppsala. Early in a career which was always characterized by initiative he developed an interest in ecological investigations of house-sites in their natural environment. He pursued this interest purposefully, concentrating through the twenties and early thirties on the field archaeology of Öland, on which he embarked with a study of burials and the lay-out of farms. He carried out the excavations himself, studying land-use, house-construction, the relation between burials and settlements; his work conveyed exciting new insights into the possibilities of archaeology. *Öland during the Early Iron Age* (*Öland under äldre järnåldern*), published in 1933, is a pioneering contribution. Numerous investigations followed upon this; one with similar objectives was the investigation of Vallhagar, on Gotland, a collaborative venture between scholars from the different Scandinavian countries, which Stenberger organized immediately after the Second World War. He was a firm believer in this type of co-operation, working with P. Nørlund in Greenland and with other Scandinavian scholars in Iceland.

Stenberger was author of a complete survey of *The Prehistory of Sweden* (*Det forntida Sverige*), a sober treatment of all the major problems. He had himself contributed in a variety of fields: from

110 M. Stenberger (1898–1973)

the Neolithic period, for instance, his work on the Stone Age village and burial-place at Västerbjers on Gotland may be mentioned. It is, however, the Viking Age that has benefited most from his studies; his monograph on the silver hoards of Gotland, an impressive assemblage of finds, provides the fullest discussion of this Scandinavian material so far available.

Many names could be added to the list of scholars discussed in this chapter, those for example whose research was devoted to Gotland.[81] This island, fortunate in its isolated position, attained to a high level of civilization in prehistoric times, as is evident from the exquisite art objects. There are, moreover, great quantities of treasure hoards. A proportionately higher number of Roman *denarii*, late Roman *solidi*, and Arabic and west-European coins of the Viking period have been found there than anywhere else in Scandinavia, a sign of Gotland's importance as a trading centre.

Among the more noteworthy early excavations is the series carried out by F. Nordin during the years around the turn of the century. As well as investigating numerous burials, he worked on Iron Age house-sites, which, under his careful scrutiny, yielded valuable new data. Later he took up the congenial task of studying the richly ornamented picture-stones of local Gotland limestone, a project which was interrupted by his death in 1920 but was later resumed by Lindqvist.

J. Nihlen carried through a number of Stone Age investigations, and – in collaboration with G. Boëthius – published a brief survey of the numerous stone-built Iron Age farmsteads on the island; moreover, he studied iron extraction. H. Hansson wrote a thesis on the Bronze Age and H. Rydh on the box-shaped fibula, a type of ornament peculiar to Gotland. Both described and classified this distinctive find-material.

Although Gotland, like Öland, held a special attraction for archaeologists, quite a number of field surveys were carried out elsewhere; there were attempts, also, to interpret the widely diffused rock engravings, which, once located, were published in a series of monographs. This was an area where such scholars as G. Hallström and Nordén made valuable contributions.

Chapter Nine

The Archaeology of Finland

111 FINNISH archaeology owes its first real progress to J.R. Aspelin, who accurately and perceptively pointed out its special problems.[82] He gave the subject academic standing and aroused the interest of the general public by forming the Finnish Society of Antiquaries (Finlands fornminnes-förening). Born in 1842 and therefore a contemporary of Müller and Montelius, Aspelin was a native of Österbotten, where his father was a pastor. But if we are to compare him with any other Scandinavian archaeologist, it ought surely to be Worsaae. They were both men of exceptional calibre, and both were motivated by Romantic ideals. Like Worsaae, Aspelin recognized that the prehistoric monuments of his country should be studied and safeguarded, and he took the initiative in the setting up of an official body, the Archaeological Commission, to take charge of these duties. He was instrumental in the formation of a large museum, which was later expanded.

111 J.R. Aspelin (1842–1915)

Aspelin's lively interest in prehistory developed out of his activity as a local historian; he had studied history at college and even after graduating in the subject in 1866, it continued to hold his attention. Information on the prehistoric period was scarce, very little work having been done on prehistoric finds. His response, logically enough, was to pay a visit to Stockholm where in 1868 he made contact with H.H. Hildebrand and Montelius, becoming a member of their progressive circle. He noticed features which the regions round the Bothnian Gulf had in common, such as ancient shorelines, now situated inland, containing Stone Age material, and comparable types of burial-mounds; these initial investigations formed the subject of a short book. When this project brought him to Stockholm again in 1871 he made a longer stay, engaging in discussions of typological method, and then went on to Copenhagen, where he formed acquaintanceships with Worsaae and Müller. This contact with Danish archaeology clearly left its mark on his work. He kept up with the exchange of views between Montelius and Müller, preferring the basis for archaeological interpretation put forward by the latter, with emphasis on such points as ethnographical comparisons. On the other hand, typology played little part in his work. First and foremost, Aspelin addressed himself to tracing the origins of the Finns and their early history.

Considerable labour was required to get antiquarian work under way and to set up a museum. Aspelin had a clear idea of how to go about these tasks. The first step, in 1870, was to form an

association of interested people, the Finnish Society of Antiquaries, with the well-known historian and poet Zacharias
Topelius as its president. One of the Society's important contributions was a periodical covering the main contemporary issues.

Aspelin argued for a registration of all prehistoric remains, and
over the first twenty-five years assistants were sent out to prepare
lists and descriptions of monuments and finds.

It was this same circle of people, as one would expect, which
gave shape to the scheme for a national museum. Aspelin again
stressed the need to assemble a representative range of finds, more
comprehensive than the University collection, which had until
then received the results of the field-work. His address to the
Society in 1874 shows how the country was situated at the time –
Finland was a Grand Duchy of Russia – and gives a good impression of both Aspelin and his objectives:

'The idea of a National Museum is an obvious consequence of an
awakened national consciousness. The nation wants to learn to
know itself and the monuments of its ancestors from bygone ages;
it wants to see the fragments that remain of their struggle for their
native soil, the culture and the future we have inherited. The
harder the struggle, the dearer is the memory of the victors. And
all these monuments which enable us to follow the struggles of our
ancestors step by step through the passing centuries on the soil of
our fatherland, belong to us, the Finnish people. We have a right
to rejoice in them and the self-respect of the people and their
regard for their monuments and the self-defence against outside
influences, even in a political sense, too.
'We must demand even more of a Finnish National Museum.
From what I have already said it should be clear that a National
Museum should aim at giving a picture of the work of the nation
and its natural activity in the service of humanity. . . . The Finnish
people is the only representative of the Finno-Ugric tribes in the
contemporary culture of the Nordic countries. . . . It is the cause
of the Finno-Ugric tribes that we are called upon to further.'[83]

Both for Aspelin's generation and for the earlier one which had had
Castrén as its intellectual leader, the Finno-Ugric idea was a great
rallying point. In the study of Finnish prehistory there was the
same interest in establishing kinship with the other regions where
Finno-Ugric languages were still spoken.

The most urgent requirement was a central museum to house
and display all the finds which had come to light, and also contain
ethnological collections, another important aspect of its work.
The Finnish student union had already begun forming such a
collection. Approaches were made to the Senate on a number of
occasions but with little success; eventually, however, this body
recognized that the scheme was a valuable one, though of the
opinion that it would have to be combined with a Bill for the protection of prehistoric finds and monuments. After lengthy discussion, an Archaeological Commission with a State Archaeologist
as secretary and administrative head was established by proclamation of the Tsar in 1883. A variety of cultural organizations
had the right to elect Commission members, and in 1885 Aspelin,
a professor since 1878, became the first State Archaeologist. A

special subcommittee immediately took up the onerous task of finding a site and an acceptable design for the museum. A building in the Classical style having been vetoed, the choice went instead to a design which allowed for later extensions and, more to the point, conformed with prevailing national-romantic ideals. The Tsar's approval was made known in 1905, the foundation-stone was laid a year later, but the actual prehistoric exhibitions were not opened to the public until 1923. Thus Aspelin, who died in 1915, never saw the full realization of his aims.

112

The significant measures of 1883 defined the responsibilities of the Archaeological Commission. Under its authority were placed all ancient monuments, whether from the prehistoric or the historic era. It was forbidden to excavate them or cause them to be disturbed without first consulting the Commission, which in this way was given control of all field-work. It was obligatory to surrender finds of prehistoric objects to the Commission, which was empowered to pay full compensation, plus twenty-five per cent, for finds it wished to purchase. In other cases the finder had the full right of disposal.

The Archaeological Commission and the post of State Archaeologist were modelled respectively on the Vitterhetsakademi and the Royal Antiquary in Stockholm; but initially the Finnish State Archaeologist was in a weaker position than his Swedish counterpart. As the sole professional prehistorian on the Commission he depended on the chairman to get his proposals submitted at meetings and had no special voting privileges. Aspelin sharply criticized the structure of the Commission, enlisting support from scholars outside Finland, among them Müller, and in 1893 he proposed a Commission membership consisting of department heads from the museum, then recently appointed, with the State Archaeologist as chairman. Funds had been allocated that year for three research posts at the museum and excavations by the Commission. Meanwhile, Aspelin's proposals were firmly rejected by the other members of the Commission; after his death, however, the plan was adopted and in the same year, 1920, the membership was increased by the addition of a lawyer to advise on legal problems. Reconstituted in this way, recognizing the importance of professional expertise in deciding antiquarian questions, the Com-

112 The National Museum of Finland, Helsinki

mission has functioned most efficiently, the main decisions being reached through discussions among the Commission members.

Aspelin's real interest was in research, and as a scholar he successfully carried out some major investigations, much to the benefit of archaeology. He wanted to assemble material which would illuminate the early stages of Finnish prehistory, and embarked on study-tours to the west and east, making a particularly lengthy stay in Moscow and St Petersburg (as Leningrad was then called) and familiarizing himself with the museums there; he also visited the larger regional museums in Russia, collecting drawings of artifacts which he thought had their origin in Finno-Ugric culture. His presentation of this ample material took the form of a profusely illustrated work, *Antiquités du Nord Finno-Ougrien*, issued in five volumes between 1877 and 1884 and containing 2,200 illustrations. Previously, in 1875, he had published a thesis titled 'The

113 Frontispiece of the third volume of Aspelin's *Antiquités du Nord Finno-Ougrien*

HELSINKI 1878.

Elements of Finno-Ugric Archaeological Research' (in Finnish);
two years later he was made a supernumerary professor. Industry
and contagious enthusiasm marked his approach to scholarship.
On finishing his book he wrote to his fiancée, Miss Anna Nielsen,
a Dane:

'It is a great work that is finished. The material consists of works
from the hands of the Finnish tribes. God has permitted me to
be the first to collect these priceless relics with such loving care.
They will testify on behalf of the Finnish tribes and free them from
being for ever placed last in the ranks of cultured and uncultured
peoples.'[84]

This was in no way an exaggeration. He had succeeded in master-
ing a large and varied assemblage of material and in classifying it
into culture areas; of these he ascribed particular significance to
Bronze Age western Siberia and the Altai. To back up this viewpoint he undertook a number of expeditions, carrying out
excavations and describing monuments in the Yenisei and
Minusinsk areas, seeking traces of his distant forbears. The inscriptions there, however, were classed as Turkish by V. Thomsen, the
Danish philologist, and as a consequence a possible Finnish background 'disappeared over the horizon', as C. A. Nordman put it.[85]
He arrived at an Early Iron Age dating for a cemetery of that period
at Ananyino, Vyatka, part of which he excavated, after taking the
Scythian parallels into consideration; this is generally accepted.

In the brief account of Finnish prehistory he published in 1885
he gave an interesting view of early developments in his own
country. He traced two cultural traditions through the Stone and
Bronze Ages, a western one whose finds showed Scandinavian
affinities and an eastern one which was closely related to finds from
the Ladoga and Onega areas. He distinguished two phases within
the Iron Age and supposed the Finnish tribes to have reached their
present home during the second of these two, through displacement by the Huns, some by way of Karelia, others from Estonia.
At the same time the Slavs, as they spread, pushed other Finnish
tribes eastwards, so splitting the Finnish people into two groups.
With finds, historical sources, loan-words, etc., as evidence, he
gave a detailed picture of the late prehistoric period – its house
remains, burial customs, social structure and means of subsistence.
Though some corrections have been necessitated by more recent
excavations, this should not lead us to underrate the stimulating
effect of his work. He created an ambiance in which scholarship
could flourish and devoted his antiquarian activities to the preservation of his country's prehistoric relics in a fine new museum.

H. Appelgren-Kivalo, one of his closest colleagues and eventual
successor, pressed on with Aspelin's schemes, supplementing them
with some of his own. He was one of those who wanted a flexible
design for the museum, and worked hard at shifting and re-
arranging its displays.

There are several reasons for his importance as a scholar. Not
only had he accompanied Aspelin on museum-tours and excavations, preparing drawings for him, but after his friend's death he
saw to the publication of some of his works, such as *Alt-Altaische
Kunstdenkmäler*. His own writings include a number of mono-

114 Reconstruction of women's clothing from the Viking period (*left*) and the early Middle Ages (*right*), found in graves in Finland. National Museum of Finland

graphs on important find-groups, among them fortified refuge-places, which he considered to be Finnish, with the exception of the examples on the Åland Islands, which have close Swedish affinities. He is best remembered, however, for his published work (1907, in German) on the distinguished research he did into Late Iron Age Finnish costume. At sites in the south-west of Finland, among them the cemetery near Överby church in Bjärnå, he painstakingly excavated this clothing and himself saw to its conservation; as a result it was possible to reconstruct accurately Viking Age and early medieval clothing fashions. He also worked 114 on finds of skis; in his stylistic studies, a type of research which occupied him throughout his career, he concentrated on contacts with the east, where his knowledge of parallels was so wide.

Of Aspelin's other collaborators, P. Th. Schwindt made a name for himself with investigations of burial-sites in Karelia, published in a dissertation titled *The Iron Age in Karelia*, which owes its importance to the way in which the numerous finds are presented.

The next generation of scholars had more chance to specialize in particular periods and topics. Its leading figures, A. Hackman and J. E. Ailio, were both men of exceptional gifts, the one shy and reserved, the other distinguished and extrovert. Hackman, who spent part of his student years in Stockholm, was influenced by the methods of Montelius and was soon attracted to problems of the Early Iron Age, but he quickly realized that typology as such could not be applied to Finnish material of the first five centuries AD, since the type-series were not fully exemplified. However, his appraisal of the finds is most capable and reliable and with this book, which appeared in thesis form in 1905, he gained recognition among European archaeologists. He had a background of

115 A. L. F. Hackman (1864–1942)

comparative studies in museums such as Stockholm, Copenhagen and those of East Prussia where he became closely acquainted with two outstanding scholars of his time, Tischler and Kemke.

In the final chapter of his book Hackman put forward a theory on the migration of the Finns which in due course was to set the trend for subsequent scholarship. Part of his evidence was the presence of Gothic loan-words in Finnish, first demonstrated by V. Thomsen.

It was Hackman's contention that the Finns had crossed the eastern Baltic lands into the west of Finland not later than the early years of the Christian era. Gothic culture in the regions adjacent to the mouth of the Vistula had its effect on them, and once settled in their new territories they came under Scandinavian influence. Tribes moved westwards into the east of Finland or Karelia in contact with their kinsfolk to the west.

It is extremely difficult to form a balanced evaluation of this use of archaeological sources to demonstrate the migration of a people defined in linguistic terms, when no contemporary linguistic evidence survives. All the same, honest and thorough reasoning enabled Hackman to make an acceptable working hypothesis of his theory. He was too busy with his museum work to do much further writing, aside from his *Atlas de Finlande* (1899), which gave an account of the finds and their distribution and was reissued in 1910, with Ailio contributing the chapter on the Stone Age.

116 J.E. Ailio (1872–1933)

Where Hackman had devoted his talents to the Iron Age, Ailio chose the Stone Age. Geology being part of his training, he was excellently qualified to work on the relationship between beach-ridges and Stone Age villages, and in 1909 he published a dissertation on the subject titled *Die steinzeitlichen Wohnplatzfunde in Finland*, a pioneering analysis of material which had previously seemed quite intractable. His work, like Hackman's, bore the impress of Montelius' training in typology, a method which the size and scope of Ailio's find-material made readily usable. As a lecturer at the University of Helsingfors in 1910, Ailio exerted much influence on the subsequent generation of archaeologists, furthering an interest in the natural sciences and in research into the earlier part of the prehistoric era, his own special field.

Yet a third young Finnish scholar, A.M. Tallgren, took up prehistoric archaeology shortly after 1900. During a stay in Sweden, he was impressed by Montelius' dynamism but soon came to feel that his own aims had more in common with the comparative, culture-historical approach characteristic of Danish archaeology, with its attention to the precise functions of prehistoric artifacts. He made his name, meanwhile, by taking up and continuing Aspelin's wide-ranging studies in Russian archaeology; his judicious grouping and comparisons made *Kupfer- und Bronzezeit in Nord- und Ostrussland*, the first volume of which appeared in 1911 as a dissertation, a work of major importance. He disagreed with Aspelin where the older scholar stressed the significance of the Altai Bronze Age for eastern Russia, and so spelt an end to the idea of the Altai as the original Finnish homeland. He pointed out the importance of the Fatyanovo culture, with its elegant Late Stone Age battle-axes and pottery, as a connecting-link between

117 A.M. Tallgren (1885–1945)

the Caucasus and central Europe. He brought his survey of the various phases of the Bronze Age and contact with the west down as far as Ananyino, a topic which he was later to take up again. Altogether, the strength of Tallgren's writings lies in the way he characterizes and compares different culture areas and not in the actual detailed study of artifacts. After a spell as lecturer and, briefly, professor at Dorpat, he applied, like Ailio, for the newly established Chair of Finnish and Scandinavian archaeology at the University of Helsingfors. As the successful candidate, Tallgren had a fresh incentive to continue his work, whereas Ailio gave up the profession entirely, after having devoted so much industry and talent to it. He went into politics and for a time was Minister of Education.

Tallgren is especially well known for having edited *Eurasia septentrionalis antiqua*, which first appeared in 1926 and continued until the beginning of the Second World War in 1939. This periodical, a point of contact for western and eastern archaeological schools, was so dependent on its editor that it died with him. Tallgren found space in it for many of his own later studies – among them a history of Finnish archaeology – but in general did his best to make it a representative organ, enlisting the co-operation of prominent European scholars. Entirely his own brainchild, this new creation left its mark, like his inspiring teaching, on scholarship in Finland.

Great advances in the understanding of the Stone Age were made at this time, thanks to Ailio's pupils. Pälsi, the most productive of them, was for a time head of the Department of Archaeology at the National Museum. He devoted his thesis to Stone Age settlements in Karelia, describing living conditions in Stone Age Finland. He had the good fortune to uncover some items of fishing equipment, of which the most noteworthy was an ancylus-period net from a bog near St Andreae in the south-east of Finland. Concentrating on the exploration of the Åland Islands, B. Cederhvarf examined the significant Stone Age village of Jettböle, where he found some sixty clay figurines.

Äyräpää who was on the staff of the Archaeological Commission, latterly as head of the Department of Prehistory, becoming a supernumerary professor in 1938, brought a keen and trained mind to the consideration of the broad spectrum of Stone Age problems. His special interest was the boat-axe culture, for which, like Müller before him, he suggested an Indo-European background. He also studied the regional development of certain areas, such as Kyrkslätt and Esbo parishes in the south of Finland, beginning with the earliest finds, simple axes, and progressing through various stages of comb-impressed pottery, boat-axe finds, and the late phase, the Kiukais culture.

C. A. Nordman, a scholar of wide interests who wrote an excellent outline history of Finnish archaeology, had a somewhat unusual career. Having studied at Helsingfors, under Ailio, he proceeded, in 1912, to Copenhagen, where Müller was quick to realize his potential and to find an opening for him at the National Museum; he stayed there until 1919, when a return to his native country was made necessary by a variety of undertakings. He

118 C. A. Nordman (1892–1972)

produced an excellent description and analysis of megalithic graves in Denmark, based in part on recent excavations, a monograph which he later followed up with a complete treatment of megalithic culture in western Europe. Taking his cue from Müller's monograph of 1884, he studied problems of archaeological method (1915) and showed that false analogies and a use of typology without reference to the wider context led to invalid interpretations. It was common at this period to identify culture areas with national types, and Scandinavian scholars were not immune from the tendency. The migrations of the Goths and the Cimbrians was a topic which never quite lost its appeal, and Kossinna revived this approach to the subject in his writings. Finland, with its two ethnic groups, was an attractive testing-ground for such theories, but Nordman cautioned against conclusions of too sweeping a kind.

Following his study of megalithic cultures in western Europe, Nordman provided fresh and original evidence of his insight into European civilization with his publication of Anglo-Saxon coins found in Finland. After 1936, as State Antiquary, he was influential in the development of antiquarian work, an instance of which being the new protection law, passed in 1963.

Until then the carefully drafted Imperial proclamation of 1883 had functioned satisfactorily, although it allowed for certain exemptions. While in principle all field-monuments were pro-tected it was open to the landowner to request their removal. Prehistoric finds, on the other hand, reverted exclusively to the State. The Archaeological Commission was empowered to accept such finds and to reimburse the finder. The new law made no change in this arrangement, and it is worth noting that it applies to objects of wood and stone as well as precious materials. The right to purchase new finds, formerly a prerogative of the National Museum, now extends to other museums.

The new law follows the example of its Swedish counterpart, adopted in 1942, in taking account of the immediate environment of a protected monument; in Finland a border at least two metres wide is scheduled along with each monument. The law as set out describes the different types of monument and it is stressed that protection measures apply to them whether registered or unknown to archaeologists. A protection order may now no longer be lifted or modified except with permission from the county administration, the highest regional authority, in consultation with the Archaeological Commission, though appeals may be made to the Ministry of Education. If an application of this sort is made by a public body in the course of major construction and the Commission rules in favour of it, the expenses of excavation must be borne by the authority concerned. This is all a distinct improvement, though certain parts of the new legislation continue to be controversial; nevertheless, tradition associated with the important measures of 1883 still plays its part.

Danish Archaeology after Müller

Long after Müller's retirement, Danish archaeology continued to bear the impress of his personality and his humanistic training. Some years passed before scholars began to open up new lines of inquiry and address themselves to new problems. When they did so it was to some extent by working independently of the National Museum, but by degrees their views gained acceptance there too and became a normal part of archaeology. With his minute investigation of house-sites and burials in Kraghede (Vendsyssel), in 1900, Th. Thomsen, who himself switched to the fields of ethnography soon after, brought work on settlements to a temporary close. His own findings were not published immediately and therefore attracted little notice. H. Kjaer began excavations at Ginderup (Thy), an important project which came to an end with his death. The team – archaeologists, botanists, a zoologist and a geologist – which had been brought together around the turn of the century to investigate shell-heaps disbanded again, each of these specialists returning to his normal work. No need was felt for a more permanent form of co-operation.

It was the National Museum, occupying a focal position in Danish archaeology, which retained the leadership. During the 1920s the head of the Department of Prehistory was C. Neergaard, a skilled excavator. He personally investigated important cemeteries, among them those in the Lisbjerg area near Aarhus, using the pottery in particular to gain new information on regional groups of the Roman Iron Age. But neither this work nor his investigation (later resumed by Th. Mathiassen) of Dyrholmen, a Stone Age settlement in Djursland, was published by him.

In 1933 he was succeeded by J. Brøndsted, a man whose in- 122 fluence would encompass every facet of archaeology: research, popularization, antiquarian work (including the adoption of a law protecting ancient monuments), university teaching, relations with the regional museums, and co-operation between the Scandinavian countries. He initiated the Scandinavian journal *Acta Archaeologica* (in English, German and French). He was a writer of distinction, rivalling Worsaae in his ability to kindle the layman's interest in his subject. An attractive picture of him emerges from his essays and memoirs; [86] his three-volume *Denmark's Prehistory* (*Danmarks Oldtid*) (1938–40) enjoyed popular acclaim, as is clear from the fact that this work has since twice been reissued, and this has benefited archaeology as a whole. The resemblance to Worsaae's book of the same title is significant.

Both books, separated by just a century, illuminate the firm cultural tradition of Denmark and the interplay between the Danish countryside and the cultural patterns of successive eras. So detailed an exposition, well illustrated and carefully documented, is witness enough to its author's power to arouse the reader's interest.

Of the three volumes, the one dealing with the Stone Age represents the most marked advance on its earlier counterpart, Müller's *Our Prehistory (Vor Oldtid)*. This was in part because Brøndsted had a longer time-span to cover, since in the years that followed the publication of Müller's book a period of the Stone Age still older than the kitchen-midden period had been discovered. At the same time, however, the problems became more complex. Evidence of the co-existence at the same period of fishing and farming cultures had been found, and the Neolithic phases had been subjected to new analysis. The lively controversies of the time are judiciously reflected in Brøndsted's text. In writing his volume on the Bronze Age he did not have to reckon with the former vigorous exchange of views. His well-balanced account rests securely on the classificatory schemes of Montelius and the finds themselves, superb as they are. He contrasted this era, so rich in remains, with the scantily attested Early Iron Age, attributing that age's poverty to initial setbacks, which later gave way to renewed progress. For the rest, his third volume drew on newly published finds, among them settlements with field-systems and the remains of houses. Here, however, he made use of a great deal of unpublished material, showing what a wealth of resources lay at hand in Danish collections.

Brøndsted's final section, on the Viking Age, is relatively brief. The period was his own speciality and later formed the subject of a separate work, where he treated the period on a broad basis. Though he made additions to this final section in subsequent editions of *Danmarks Oldtid* it was impossible to do justice to such an eventful era in a general work. Originally trained in classical philology and art history, he had in fact gone into archaeology out of an interest in Viking Age problems. His thesis 'Early English Ornament' (1924), which appeared in expanded form in English translation, was a brilliant piece of work. In it he discussed the different Scandinavian styles and pointed out to what extent they were known in England, while also giving a fine account of Anglo-Saxon art and its debt to Syrian-Coptic motifs (interlace work, vine patterns, etc.) and of insular influence on Scandinavian art. Full of acute observation, it can still be studied to advantage, though some questions have been approached in a different way by subsequent writers.

The impact of Brøndsted's scholarship was not solely the result of his large output of published work but in large measure also of his university teaching. Originally it was Worsaae who had forged this link between research and teaching, while Müller had briefly attempted to keep it up, only to renounce it shortly afterwards. Brøndsted served for several years as a lecturer before being appointed to a Chair in Scandinavian Archaeology and European Prehistory in 1941. Then, in 1950, the National Museum welcomed

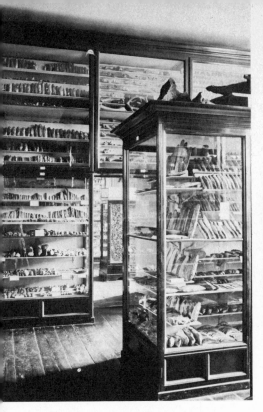

him back, this time as its head – a post which after some years carried with it the title of 'State Antiquary', an indication of the wider responsibilities of the post. His original aim was to create an atmosphere of fruitful interplay between research and teaching within the framework of the National Museum. For the small group of students who had come into this newly established field since the close of the twenties there were now fresh opportunities to participate in excavations, not to mention the massive task of enlarging the National Museum, which called for much voluntary labour. The whole block behind the Prince's Palace now constituted the new museum buildings. The exhibitions, as first shown in 1937, were unostentatious and much enlarged; there was sufficient storage space to hold the fruits of several years of further excavations.

Relations between the National Museum and the provincial museums improved markedly during Brøndsted's term as inspector, and local initiative enabled several museums of cultural history, which were expanding and eager to exhibit archaeological finds, to engage professional staff. There were still certain restrictions on excavations. However, a ministerial circular of 1941 introduced a regulation stating that in cases where large-scale investigations came within the catchment area of a regional museum, the National Museum and the regional museum concerned should keep each other informed about the commencement of the project and the progress they were making with it.

In the course of a few years State grants were raised, the museums acquired staff with an academic training and their independence was officially codified. Significant progress was now made,

119 Exhibition of Stone Age finds from the beginning of this century in the National Museum, Copenhagen

120 A display at the National Museum in the 1930s: Iron Age weapons recovered from bogs

119, 120

though not on a planned basis, since proposals for new regional museums depended entirely on local initiative. In turn, the National Museum was relieved of some of the numerous rescue excavations it had had to carry out. In the thirties, however, not enough of these large museums had emerged to provide any real help with the new antiquarian duties brought into being by the adoption of the protection law, passed by the Rigsdag in 1937. Under it all existing ancient monuments were protected and put in the custody of the National Museum. Although it would have been feasible to enact special antiquarian legislation, as elsewhere in Scandinavia, and to apply to archaeological finds the same provisions as to monuments, it was decided to keep the ancient Danefae law in practice. Over the centuries flint objects had been discovered by the hundreds and retained by their finders. That they should have gone to the museums never occurred to anyone, and new regulations to this effect were bound to cause resentment. On the other hand, there had been general respect for the law of Danefae concerning objects made of precious metal, and this could be applied in certain cases to rare objects where metal value did not come into question.

It was left to the National Museum to decide which monuments should be legally protected and what the exact size of the protected area should be. Since 1892 the museum had been the body officially responsible for the preservation of monuments, and excavations depended on the co-operation of the very landowners who had ancient examples on their property. A policy of cautious diplomacy was, therefore, called for. In the event the law was favourably received; over the years it was extensively revised, so as to take into account the monument's surroundings. The immediate environs of monuments were safeguarded from road or building construction, though an applicant might appeal to regional authorities and to the National Museum. The chairmen of these regional authorities, who are judges, were entrusted with the actual task of inspection until the law was newly revised in 1970. More than twenty thousand prehistoric monuments are now protected, being officially recorded in the title deeds of the properties where they were situated, but those which had been ploughed over – a number several times as large – were still not legally protected or reserved in any way for professional investigation. The last revision of the law provides for this eventuality by stating that any discoveries of archaeological finds or monuments must be reported to the State Antiquary, who then takes responsibility for them. This 1970 legislation not only separated the functions of State Antiquary and National Museum but created a new administrative unit to handle statutory antiquarian work. This body co-operates with museums and the university institutes in assigning these excavations.

Even if it meant a redistribution of the combined load of museum work and antiquarian duties which had rested on the National Museum for eighty years, the antiquarian authority and the museums in Denmark continued their close collaboration.

The Royal Society of Nordic Antiquaries had worked in association with the museum under Worsaae and again under

Müller, and with Brøndsted the same relationship continued.

Th. Mathiassen, Brøndsted's closest colleague, was by contrast an archaeologist whose reputation rested on his field-work.[87] While still a child he had witnessed the investigation of the Stone Age settlement at Maglemose (near Mullerup), discovered by his father. During his student years Mathiassen followed this example by exploring for further Stone Age sites. With a science degree behind him he went to the Arctic, taking part in Knud Rasmussen's fifth Thule expedition, as the archaeologist of the party. He devoted his time first and foremost to investigating vestiges of hunting culture, related to the Stone Age remains of Denmark. He gained an insight into the living conditions of a hunting society. In his methodical analytical work on the early central Eskimo cultures he gave prominence to the early Thule culture (contemporary with the Viking Age in Scandinavia), tracing it from Siberia to the east of Greenland. This monograph, which he followed up with further reports on excavations in Greenland, gained him a doctorate in 1927.

Mathiassen came to the National Museum when Brøndsted was appointed head of the Department of Prehistory and at once embarked industriously on his explorations into the earliest Danish cultures. In the mid-thirties he and his student assistants were engaged in reconnaissance expeditions along river banks in central Jutland, searching for Early Stone Age settlements. The Klosterlund site, which represents an early phase of the Maglemose culture, when Jutland and England were part of the same land mass, was investigated. In 1937 the investigation of Dyrholmen was resumed. Distribution patterns within the settlement, which had gradually shifted position as the water level grew lower, revealed that it contained three phases of the Ertebølle culture. The lowest, and therefore the most recent, of these represented a stage of the Ertebølle culture contemporary with neolithic settlements, so confirming the ideas put forward by Rydbeck ten years before. Even older than Klosterlund was the Bromme site in central Zealand, which owes its discovery to E. Westerby, author of a careful report on a site representative of the early Ertebølle culture at Klampenborg, near Copenhagen. Thanks to the expert co-operation of archaeologists and scientists, settlements from late glacial times had now been identified, whereas previously there had only been the sporadic traces of nomadic hunting tribes to work on.

Mathiassen devoted his last years to the investigation of the settlement pattern in two representative regions, the west of Jutland and north-west Zealand. Both these detailed reports found prompt publication, with analyses which took their cue from Müller's topographical work.

H.C. Broholm, another contemporary, was a Bronze Age specialist. The subject of his dissertation was the later part of this period, and the successive pottery styles represented. He devoted a monograph to a survey of Bronze Age finds. Broholm is best remembered for his painstaking work on the significant Skrydstrup burial and the other Bronze Age clothing finds (here capably assisted by M. Hald, an expert on textiles), as well as for his

121

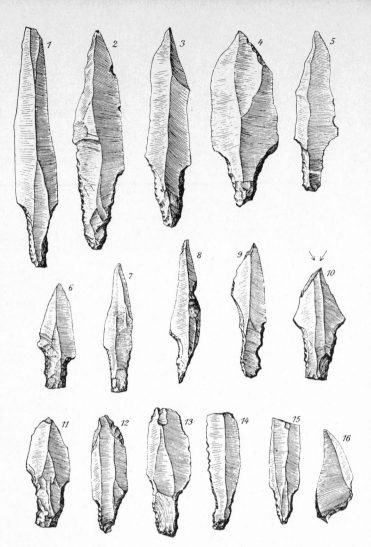

121 Tanged arrow-heads from Bromme, Zealand. Early post-glacial period

publication of the strange long trumpets of the Bronze Age, known as 'lurer'.

Throughout this period G. Hatt was exploring the field of Iron Age agriculture and settlements. A trained ethnographer, he left the National Museum for a Chair in the Department of Geography. The house-building and life-style of prehistoric peoples were two of his chief interests. He gave prominence to the ecological aspects of the subject, investigating the natural surroundings within which house-sites were found as well as the man-made embankments in fields. His primary aim was to find deserted villages of the Iron Age; he judiciously chose for his reconnaissance expeditions such areas as Himmerland (north Jutland) and in western Jutland, Nørre Fjand. The last-mentioned area was especially important, providing information on living conditions. The copious material which he collected appeared in a popular book, *Agriculture in Prehistoric Denmark*, and in scholarly publications. In his interpretations the sociological aspect is stressed; transverse field embankments, for example, he explained as pointing to the splitting up of land among several heirs.

Like Hatt, K. Friis Johansen was active first at the National Museum and later at the University. He is remembered for his thorough excavation and publication of the Svaerdborg settlement, which in minor ways differs from Maglemose, and for his excellent account of the Hoby burial, which contained the richest assemblage of imported objects so far discovered in Scandinavia. The splendid bronze vessels and two exquisite silver bowls, adorned with scenes from Homer, together with the other treasures, are unique in northern Europe for their quality. Friis Johansen postulated that they might have come directly from a Roman aristocrat in the north-east of Gaul.

It was a no less fruitful period for amateur archaeologists. One of the most noteworthy was J. Winther, a Rudkøbing merchant, who founded his town's museum, endowing it with a wealth of finds. An exuberant character, he had a gift for choosing important sites for his excavations. Though he retained fond memories of his meeting, as a young man, with Worsaae, whose kindness made a great impression on him, it was under the liberal dispensation of Brøndsted that his own work flourished. Among his achievements was the investigation of important neolithic settlements, some with house-sites, at Lindø, Troldebjerg and Blandebjerg, each representative of a significant phase in the prehistory of Langeland.

An Odense amateur, Helweg-Mikkelsen, chemist and chairman of the local museum's board, was responsible for the discovery of the Viking ship burial at Ladby, near Kerteminde in north Funen. Following the excavation of this major find, a vault resembling the original barrow was built over the scanty remains – nails showing the shape of the ship and the few finds which had not been lost to tomb-robbers. G. Rosenberg, a conservator of the National Museum, did the actual excavation; he was not new to this type of investigation, having uncovered the collapsed remains of a vessel dating from the Roman Iron Age at Hjortspring, on Als.

Though the Viking Age has some claim to be considered a part of the historical era, it has been the convention in Scandinavia to class it as prehistory. Among the specialists of various interrelated disciplines, P. Nørlund, a medievalist and sometime Director of 122
the National Museum, demonstrated by his remarkable excavation that Trelleborg, a circular stronghold near Slagelse in 123
Zealand, owed its construction to the Vikings. Between 1934 and 1942, he uncovered the carefully designed, barrack-like houses. Nørlund's detailed monograph of 1948 places the building of the

122 J. Brøndsted and P. Nørlund having a discussion at the National Museum during the winter of 1940–41

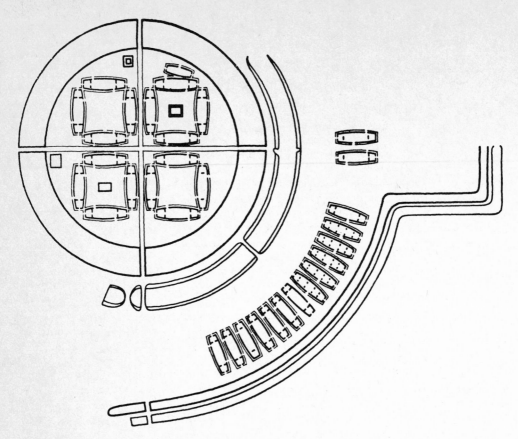

123 Plan of Trelleborg. (After
P. Nørlund)

stronghold at around the year AD 1000 and relates it to the powerful
position the Danish royal house held at this time, an interpretation
which was reinforced by the discovery of two more round forts.
These sites, Aggersborg (near Limfjord) and Fyrkat (in east
Jutland) were explored by Nørlund's talented assistant C.G.
Schultz, whose work was cut short by his early death.

Jelling, the seat of the Viking dynasty, was a perennial source of
fascination to archaeologists. After fresh work there, E. Dyggve
established that beneath the church and also in the churchyard
there were clear indications of some kind of special lay-out. He
was able to prove conclusively that the southernmost barrow on
the site did not contain a burial-chamber. Moreover, he noticed
two converging lines of stones, which seemed to point to the
presence of a heathen temple, seeing that in the churchyard there
were more stones of the same sort, which had clearly been part of
a large stone circle. His work inside the church revealed traces of
older structures whose nature became more evident with subsequent excavations, the most recent of which have provided
other possible interpretations of the site.

Parallel to the Danish border and just south of it run the
fortification walls of Danevirke and Kovirke; these too had received
scholarly attention in previous centuries. The fact that this defensive
embankment faced south showed that it owed its construction to
the Danes. Consequently Vilh. la Cour pointed out correspon-
dences between Kovirke and moats in the Viking round fortifica-

tions of the Trelleborg type, concluding that they belonged to the same period.

The colonization of Iceland falls within the Viking Age, and it is for this reason that that important Atlantic island has been so little discussed in the earlier periods; only in our own generation has a comprehensive publication of the finds been undertaken. Yet the discovery in Iceland of a closed find of Roman coins seems to presuppose contact as early as the Roman Iron Age; it may be that Iceland is the Thule of which vague descriptions occur in Classical Latin sources.

In 1939 scholars came together from all over Scandinavia to excavate deserted farms in Þjórsárdalur. A few of these farmsteads, buried by an eruption of the volcano Hekla in the Middle Ages, proved to date back to the Viking period. Clearly the same is true of other house-sites in Iceland, but the best source of information on the Scandinavian settlers on the island is in fact the grave-finds. Since close contact was naturally maintained with western Scandinavian countries, the British Isles also left their mark on early Icelandic culture. In addition to excavating some of these finds and describing them in detail, K. Eldjarn has played a major part in the formation of a new museum, vividly recreating the prehistory of Iceland for his fellow-countrymen. These and other contributions have earned him his country's highest office.

Nørlund's work led to intensified research on the part of Danish archaeologists into the original Scandinavian settlements in Greenland. Most of the structures so far uncovered are of medieval origin, but in recent years the ground plans of Viking Age farmsteads, such as Brattahlið, have been brought to light. At Brattahlið the remains of a rudimentary turf church were also discovered. With these investigations, however, we enter the post-war years and the gradual rise of a new generation.

Epilogue: Models in Archaeology

THE study of Scandinavian archaeology grew out of centuries of antiquarian speculations. By recognizing the value of material sources C.J. Thomsen defined the new discipline, making it independent of literary, philological and folkloristic studies.[88] Proudly he stated: 'A tumulus, a stone circle in the countryside, a stone tool, or a metal ornament unearthed from the sequestered burial chamber – all these afford us a more vivid picture of the prehistoric age than Saxo or Snorri, the *Eddas* or Tacitus' *Germania*.'[89] He proclaimed the self-sufficiency of archaeology, and with his technological model of the three ages – stone, bronze and iron – put archaeology on a systematic footing. While earlier scholarship had to some degree anticipated this model, he was the first to realize and fully elaborate it about 1820. This constituted the first decisive step in advancing archaeological theories. Another was soon to be taken, this time on the other side of Öresund, at the University of Lund. Nilsson – who had an able predecessor in Stobaeus, the eighteenth-century scholar – pointed out that the artifacts indicated specific life styles which could be reconstructed by using ethnographical parallels. The idea was taken up by Worsaae and further elaborated in his book *Danmarks Oldtid* (1843). Within the evolutionary schema proposed by Nilsson for early societies – savages, nomads and farming communities – the people of the Stone Age corresponded to savages, that is to hunting and fishing communities. Worsaae[90] made wide use of reports from Greenland, America, the South Sea islands and other regions, bringing the Stone Age vividly to life with a series of parallels. One of his sources was the communications of the scientist P.W. Lund on life in a primitive community near Lagoa Santa, in the remote heart of Brazil, where polished stone axes were known. Lund's description of the techniques in felling and hollowing-out trees, using axes and live embers,[91] was reproduced almost word for word in the Stone Age section of *Danmarks Oldtid*.[92] Though he realized that even in the late Stone Age some farming was being carried on, Worsaae argued that such an economy became general only in the Bronze Age, when metal came into use and woven fabrics replaced animal skins as clothing. Further evolution and new ornamental forms attended the introduction of iron.

A standard way of explaining cultural changes of this sort was to assume that a new tribe had invaded the territory. This trend, general among these early antiquaries, Nilsson carried to extremes, identifying the bearers of Scandinavian Stone Age culture as Lapps (whose home has always been the far North) and ascribing the introduction of the Bronze and Iron Ages to, respectively, Baal-worshippers from Phoenicia and worshippers of the Æsir.[93]

As the years passed, this model of cultural change was re-examined and took on a new form: in Worsaae's exposition change is attributable to cultural displacement,[94] an instance being the northward spread of Bronze Age culture from the Orient and southern Europe towards Scandinavia, with a base in a mineral-rich and independent central Europe. In this form the model was adopted and further refined, with the use of a great quantity of illustrative material, by Montelius and Müller and was invoked to counter the interpretations of the Kossinna school.

The close co-operation with scientists which began in the middle of the nineteenth century resulted in a better understanding of the relationship between early man and nature. By studying the remains of animals, trees, etc. at the sites and in the bogs, the scientists determined the impact of man on his surroundings and his probable way of life. The programme was clearly set out in 1869 after years of stimulating – though not always harmonious – co-operation on the part of the first kitchen-midden commission, by one of its members, J. Steenstrup,[95] and it was successfully taken over by the second commission of 1893, which supplied evidence of a basic nature.[96] In this way a most useful tradition was established in Scandinavia.

Ideas like those we have discussed came into their own gradually, at times under the strong influence of scholarship elsewhere in Europe. They ultimately reached an international audience through translations, such as for example the German and English editions of both Thomsen's *Ledetraad* and Worsaae's *Danmarks Oldtid*. Of later books, the second (1868) edition of Nilsson's *Skandinaviska Nordens Ur-Invånare* (in English) and monographs of a detailed and methodical kind, especially those of Montelius and Müller, appeared in translation and were widely discussed by readers outside Scandinavia.

From the first tentative steps of Renaissance times, official control over prehistoric remains has steadily grown more effective. As early as 1555 Olaus Magnus argued in favour of protecting ancient monuments efficaciously. In Sweden antiquaries and administrators established their position firmly in the seven-teenth century with an assertion of the Crown's exclusive title to prehistoric finds and monuments; in reality, however, the law was not strictly enforced, in that objects of relatively little value were disregarded. Finnish and Norwegian law calls unequivocally for the surrender of all prehistoric finds, whatever their value. Denmark, where the medieval law of Danefæ still continues in use, was at one time fairly lenient towards common finds like flint axes, but the newly adopted legislation of 1970 provides for compulsory notification and eventual surrender to the authorities of all archaeological finds.

Antiquarian administrators acquired their powers under a wide variety of provisions. The policy of keeping civil service supervision of antiquities distinct from museum responsibilities is traditional in Sweden and has been followed in Finland as well.

124 The runic inscription on this monument reads: 'Antiqua serva' – 'tend to the relics of the past'. From Olaus Magnus' *Historia de gentibus septentrionalibus*, 1555

A similar monuments service was instituted by Denmark in 1847 with Worsaae as active director, but the National Museum took over these statutory functions upon its establishment in 1892. This arrangement persisted until 1970, when the two functions were once more separated. A certain amount of decentralization has gone on, but it has not been carried as far as in Norway, where the five major museums, each with its own large catchment area, have the dual responsibility of housing finds and protecting field-monuments.

Cartographical surveys of antiquities also gradually reached completion. The first was the survey of Denmark from 1873, directed by Worsaae, and very detailed maps of Swedish antiquities, for instance, are being produced on the basis of air photographs.

The process by which formal connections grew up between archaeology and the universities has a different history in each country. In Sweden proposals of this sort were put forward as early as the 1600s, but regular courses in prehistoric archaeology did not begin until the mid-nineteenth century. The first actual university teacher in the discipline was Worsaae, who lectured at the University of Copenhagen from 1855 until 1866. In 1875 a Chair was established at Oslo, to which Rygh was appointed; soon after, in 1878, Aspelin was made a professor at Helsingfors. As with Worsaae, however, appointment to an administrative post meant an end to his teaching. Neither Aspelin nor Worsaae had any immediate successor: at Helsingfors the Chair was not re-established until 1921, and Copenhagen did not have one until 1941. Turning to Sweden, there have been Chairs in archaeology at Lund and Uppsala since 1919 and 1914 respectively, following some years of teaching Nordic archaeology earlier in this century. More recent are those at Aarhus, Bergen, Göteberg and Tromsø.

As we review the history of Scandinavian archaeology it is remarkable how, in the face of political animosity between the countries from the seventeenth to the early nineteenth century, antiquaries consistently upheld the value of scholarly co-operation. In their pioneer work on a heritage which all Scandinavians hold in common, personalities like Hadorph and Thomsen expressed a strong affinity with like-minded students wherever they belonged in Scandinavia, and made no secret of working in partnership with them.

It was natural, therefore, that the steadily increasing number of Scandinavian archaeologists wished to meet at regular intervals.[97] After a while conservation specialists and student bodies organized similar gatherings.

Since 1916 regular archaeologists' meetings have been held for the promotion of the common work, at which views are exchanged and recent discoveries presented. They began in a spirit of family gatherings around the grand figures of Müller and Montelius and they still maintain a touch of intimacy which is part of the tradition that has grown up around these antiquarian studies.

Notes on the Text

Abbreviation: *Aarbøger*   *Aarbøger for nordisk Oldkyndighed og Historie,* Copenhagen (also in Bibliography)

1 V. Hermansen, 1954, p. 224.
2 B. Thordeman, 1945, p. 189.
3 *Sakses Danesaga*, 1911, p. 23.
4 J. Svennung, 1967, where the subject is treated in detail.
5 G. Albeck, 1959, p. 117.
6 Olavus Petri, IV, 1917 (the original written in the 1630s was not printed but distributed in manuscript form).
7 G. Albeck, 1959, p. 117.
8 H. Schück, 1932, p. 68.
9 Ole Worm, 1965, p. 167.
10 H. Schück, 1932, p. 40. E. Svärdström, 1936. O. Almgren, 1931, p. 28.
11 Ole Worm, 1641, 1643.
12 Ole Worm, 1965, p. 174.
13 Ole Worm, 1967, p. 55.
14 Ole Worm, 1967, p. 481.
15 Ole Worm, 1643, p. 7.
16 Ole Worm, 1643, p. 110.
17 Ole Worm, 1965, p. 103.
18 Ole Worm, 1655, p. 74.
19 Ole Worm, 1968, p. 451 (cf. p. 446). Icelandic report on stone spear-point from Greenland: Ole Worm, 1967, p. 475 (cf. 1968, p. 28).
20 Ole Worm, 1967, p. 208.
21 T. Hindenburg, 1859, p. 54.
22 C. Neergaard, 1916, p. 1836.
23 H. Schück, 1932–44. A detailed survey of the Academy's history until 1837, containing a general reference to early Swedish antiquarian studies.
24 O. Rudbeck, 1937, p. 81, Tab. III, Figs 4–5. S. Lindqvist, 1930 (a), p. 249 and 1930 (b).
25 L. Holberg, 1744, p. 525.
26 B. Thordeman, 1945, p. 189.
27 G. Galster, 1946, p. 105.
28 V. Nielsen, 1949, p. 65.
29 S. Müller, 1897, p. 160.
30 P. Syv, 1787, Preface part 8, etc.
31 E. Pontoppidan, 1763, p. 110.
32 K. Stobaeus, 1738, p. 156. O. Rydbeck, 1943, p. 16.
33 A. Nordén, 1942.
34 Sv. Marstrander, 1948, p. 54.
35 J. Jensen, 1970, p. 18.

36 C. A. Nordman, 1968, p. 11. A. M. Tallgren, 1936, p. 199.
37 H. P. Anchersen, 1745. H. Lund, 1965, p. 55.
38 P. T. Wandall, 1783, p. 27.
39 C. Elling, 1942.
40 O. Klindt-Jensen, 1970, p. 14.
41 T. Hindenburg, 1859, p. 149. A. Rasmussen, 1925, p. 133. V. Hermansen, 1949, p. 38.
42 V. Hermansen, 1953, p. 157; 1931, p. 265 gives a detailed survey of these developments.
43 E. C. Werlauff, 1858. J. Brøndsted, 1954, p. 28.
44 V. Hermansen, 1953, p. 171.
45 See especially T. Hindenburg, 1859, p. 47. B. Hildebrand, 1937, p. 242.
46 B. Hildebrand, 1937, p. 337.
47 O. Klindt-Jensen, 1958 (a), p. 124, and (b), p. 145. C. J. Thomsen and F. Magnussen, 1827, p. 64.
48 Prince Christian Frederik, 1827, p. 379.
49 C. F. Herbst, 1848, p. 336.
50 M. Malmer, 1963, p. 76.
51 K. Madsen, J. Th. Lundbye, 1949, p. 66.
52 The period is discussed in detail by B. Hildebrand, 1937, pp. 189, 555, etc.
53 B. Hougen, 1961, p. 11.
54 W. Slomann, 1964, p. 5.
55 G. Kossack, 1969, p. 51.
56 A. M. Tallgren, 1936, p. 203. C. A. Nordman, 1968, p. 15.
57 No detailed biography of Worsaae exists. Important material is found in J. J. A. Worsaae, 1930 (letters, ed. Ad. Clement), 1934 (memoirs, ed. V. Hermansen) and 1938 (letters, ed. V. Hermansen); Carl S. Petersen, 1938, p. 85 refers to Worsaae's youthful polemics. Memorial speech by S. Müller, 1886, p. 1.
58 K. Thorvildsen, 1946, p. 76.
59 Queen Gunhild and Runamo: Carl S. Petersen, 1938, p. 85.
60 Carl S. Petersen, 1938,

p. 167.
61 J. J. A. Worsaae, 1849, p. 390.
62 Carl S. Petersen, 1938, p. 215. M. Ørsnes, 1969, p. xiii. J. J. A. Worsaae, 1867, p. 1.
63 J. J. A. Worsaae, 1877, p. 14.
64 J. J. A. Worsaae, 1877, p. 22.
65 M. Ørsnes, 1969, p. v.
66 P. V. Glob, 1970, p. 22.
67 O. Klindt-Jensen, 1958, p. 115.
68 H. Hildebrand, 1872–80, p. 178.
69 N. F. B. Sehested, 1884, p. 1.
70 *Nordisk Tidskrift*, 1972, p. 1 (T. J. Arne, S. Reinach, G. Kossinna, H. Kjaer, H. Shetelig, R. Sernander, A. Bugge, H. Olrik, E. Reuterskiöld). T. J. Arne, 1944, p. 69. B. Nerman, 1944, p. 5. On H. Hildebrand: B. Hildebrand, 1943, p. 95.
71 *Aarbøger*, 1934, p. 1. E. Nordman, 1960 gives a vivid picture of life in the Prince's Palace.
72 B. Hougen, 1954, p. 33, and H. Gjessing, 1920, p. 161 provide valuable assessments of Rygh's work and of his and the next generation's contributions. Cf. A. W. Brøgger, 1929, p. 28.
73 G. Gjessing, 1954, p. 1. Th. Sjøvold, 1953, p. 7.
74 A. W. Brøgger, 1929, p. 9.
75 B. Hougen, 1954, p. 34.
76 H. Shetelig, 1938, p. 342.
77 B. Hougen, 1954, p. 38.
78 W. Slomann, 1955, p. v. K. Shetelig, 1964, p. 39.
79 S. Grieg, 1953, p. v.
80 B. Schönbäck, 1958, p. 5.
81 B. Nerman, 1941.
82 A. M. Tallgren, 1936, p. 207. C. A. Nordman, 1968, p. 20.
83 C. A. Nordman, 1968, p. 24.
84 C. A. Nordman, 1968, p. 33.
85 C. A. Nordman, 1968, p. 34.
86 J. Brøndsted, 1940, p. 158 (cf. *Rast undervejs*, Copenhagen, 1942, p. 102).
87 C. J. Becker, 1968, p. 4.
88 Glyn Daniel, 1971, p. 140.

89	C.J. Thomsen, 1836, p. 27.	94	J.J.A. Worsaae, *Aarbøger*,
90	S. Nilsson, 1866, p. 1.		1872, p. 373.
91	P.W. Lund, 1838–9, p. 159.	95	J. Steenstrup, 1870, p. 336.
92	J.J.A. Worsaae, 1843, p. 11.	96	A.P. Madsen, S. Müller,
93	S. Nilsson, 1866, p. 131.		C. Neergaard, C.G.J.

Petersen, E. Rostrup, K.J.V. Steenstrup, W. Winge, *Affaldsdynger fra Stenalderen i Danmark*, Copenhagen, 1900. 97 M. Stenberger, 1963, p. 5.

Photographic Acknowledgments

ATA, Riksantikvarieämbetet, Stockholm, 2, 6, 7, 8, 23, 25, 26, 32, 55, 56, 57, 76, 77, 96, 98, 100, 101, 108; Bornholms Museum, Rønne, 69; Gunnar Eriksson, 27; P.V. Glob, 110; Det Kongelige Bibliotek, Copenhagen, 39; Kunstakademiets Bibliotek, Copenhagen, 34; Lunds Universitets Historiska Museum, 104; E. Moltke, 11, 12; National Museum, Copenhagen, 14, 37, 42, 44, 45, 48, 63, 64, 74, 75, 119, 120; National Museum, Helsinki, 111, 112, 114, 115, 116, 117, 118; Politikens Presse Foto, 122; Statens Museum for Kunst, Copenhagen, 38; Svenska Porträttarkivet, National Museum, Stockholm, 33; Universitetets Oldssaksamling, Oslo, 58, 88, 89, 90, 91, 92, 95; University Museum of Scandinavian Antiquities, Uppsala, 97.

Bibliography

'Ad Patriam Illustrandam', *Hyllningsskrift till Sigurd Curman*. Uppsala, 1946.

ALBECK, G. *Humanister i Jylland*. Copenhagen 1959, p. 117.

ALMGREN, O. 'Om tillkamsten av 1630 års antikvarie-institution', *Riksantikvarieämbetets 300-årsjubileum*. Stockholm, 1931, p. 28.

— *Sveriges fasta fornlämningar från hednatiden*,[3] Kap. III Historik. Uppsala, 1934.

ANCHERSEN, H. P. *Herthadal ved Leyre i Siaeland og det gamle Danmark 150 Aar før og efter Christi Fødsel*. Copenhagen 1745.

ARBMAN, H. 'Hjalmar Stolpe som fornforskare'. *Fornvännen* 36, 1941, p. 146.

ARNE, T. J. 'Oscar Montelius. Till hundraårsminnet av hans födelse'. *Scandia* XVI, 1944, p. 69. (v. Montelius).

— 'Antikvitetskollegiets och Antikvitetsarkivets Samlingar', *Riksantikvarieämbetets 300-årsjubileum*. Stockholm, 1931, p. 48.

ARNKIEL, M. T. *Cimbrische Heyden-Religion*. Hamburg 1702.

BECKER, C. J. 'Therkel Mathisassen og dansk arkaeologi'. *Aarbøger* 1968, p. 4.

BERING-LIISBERG, H. C. *Kunstkammeret. Dets Stiftelse og aeldste Historie*. Copenhagen 1897.

BOYE, V. *Veiledning til Udgravning af Oldsager og deres foreløbige Behandling*. Aarhus 1874.

— *Fund af Egekister fra Bronzealderen i Danmark*. Copenhagen 1896.

BROHOLM, H. C. 'Skibssaetninger i Danmark', *Fra Nationalmuseets Arbejdsmark* 1937, s. 11.

BRØGGER, A. W. 'Nasjonen og fortiden', *Universitetets oldsakssamlings Skrifter* II. Oslo 1929.

— 'Fortid og fremtid'. *Universitetets oldsakssamlings årbok* 1929. Oslo 1930.

BRØNDSTED, J. *Ved Kilderne, Strejftog i dansk Arkaeologi og Natur*. Copenhagen 1940.

— 'Nordisk Arkaeologi'. *Videnskaben i Dag*, Copenhagen 1944, p. 385.

— *Guldhornene*. Copenhagen 1954.

— 'Oldtidsminderne i Kunsten'. *Nationalmuseets Arbejdsmark* 1958, p. 5.

— Memorial speeches by P. V. Glob, N. Cleve, S. Dahl, K. Eldjárn, B. Hougen and H. Arbman. *Aarbøger* 1966, p. 5.

CHRISTIAN FREDERIK (VIII), PRINCE (later King of Denmark) 'Om Oldtidsminderne paa Bornholm og nogle der fundne Oldsager'. *Antiqvariske Annaler* 4, 1827, p. 379.

DANIEL, GLYN E. *A Hundred Years of Archaeology*. London 1950.

— *The Idea of Prehistory*. London 1962.

— *The Origin and Growth of Archaeology*. Harmondsworth 1967.

— 'From Worsaae to Childe: The Models of Prehistory'. *Proc. of the Prehistoric Society* XXXVII, 1971, p. 140.

EGGERS, H. J. *Einführung in die Vorgeschichte*. Munich 1959.

ELLING, CHR. *Den romantiske Have*. Copenhagen 1942.

Finlands författningssamling 1963 no. 395. 'Lag om fornminnen', 17 June 1963.

FREDERIK VII, KING OF DENMARK *Om Bygningsmaaden af Oldtidens Jaettestuer*. Copenhagen 1862.

GALSTER, G. 'Forordningerne af 1737 og 1752 om Danefae'. *Nordisk numismatisk årsskrift* 1946, p. 105.

GJESSING, G. 'Ingvald Undset 1853–1893–1953'. *Det kgl. Norske Videnskabers Selskabs forhandlinger* 27, 1954, p. 1.

GJESSING, H. *Arkeologien. Norsk historisk videnskap i femti år 1869–1919*, p. 161. Christiania 1920.

GLOB, P. V. *Højfolket*. Copenhagen 1970.

— *Fortidens spor. Dyrehaven og Jaegersborg Hegn*. Copenhagen 1973.

GRIEG, S. 'A. W. Brøgger'. *Viking* XVI, 1953 p. V.

HANSEN, H. P. 'Vendsyssels historiske Museum i Hjørring 1889–1939'. *Sprog og Kulter* VIII, 1939, p. 1.

HERBST, C. F. 'Hvidegaards Fundet'. *Annaler for nordisk Oldkyndighed*, 1848, p. 336.

HERMANSEN, V. 'Oprettelsen af "Den kongelige Commission til Oldsagers Opbevaring" i 1807'. *Aarbøger* 1931, p. 265.

— 'Frederik Münter og den danske Oldranskning'. *Frederik Münter et Mindeskrift* I, 2. Copenhagen 1949, s. 38.

— 'Baggrunden for Oldsagskommissionen'. *Aarbøger* 1953, p. 157.

— 'Fortidsminder og Kuriositeter i Danmarks Middelalder'. *Aarbøger* 1954, p. 220.

HILDEBRAND, B. *C. J. Thomsen och hans lärda förbindelser i Sverige 1816–1837. Bidrag till den nordiska forn- och hävda-forskningen historia, Kungl. Vitterhets historie och antikvitets akad. handl.* 44, 1. Stockholm 1937.

— 'Hans Hildebrand. Till hundraårsminnet'. *Scandia* XV, 1943, p. 95.

HILDEBRAND, B. E. 'Atgärder i äldre og senaste tid vidtagna till skyld för fäderneslandets fornlemningar'. *Antiqvarisk tidsskrift för Sverige* I, 1864, p. 1.

HILDEBRAND, H. H. 'Bidrag till spännets historia'. *Antiqvarisk tidskrift för Sverige* 4, 1872–80, p. 15.

HINDENBURG, T. 'Bidrag til den danske Archaeologis Historie'. *Dansk Maanedsskrift*, Ny Raekke I, 2–3 vols., p. 1. Copenhagen 1859.

HOLBERG, L. *Moralske Tanker* (Copenhagen 1744), ed. F. J. Billeskov Jansen. Copenhagen 1943.

HOUGEN, B. *Fra Samling til Museum. Oprindelsen til Samlingen af nordiske Oldsager*. Universitetets oldsakssamling, Oslo 1961.

— 'Fra norsk arkeologis historie'. *Viking* XVIII, 1954 p. 29.

JANSEN, J. *Beskrivelse over de paa Bornholm foranstaltede Udgravninger 1820* (in the Royal Library, Copenhagen; copy in Nationalmuseet 1. dep., Copenhagen).

JENSEN, JØRGEN 'Forhistoriens historie'. *Skalk* 1970, 4, p. 18.

KIVIKOSKI, E., 'A. M. Tallgren'. *Eurasia Septentionalis Antiqva* 1954, p. 77.

KLINDT-JENSEN, O. 'Oldgranskere, fortidsminder og rokkesten på Bornholm'. *Nationalmuseets Arbejdsmark* 1958a, p. 107.

— 'Udgravninger på Bornholm 1816–24'. *Bornholmske Samlinger* XXXVI, 1958b, p. 145.

— 'Danmarks oldtid og dansk arkaeologi'. *Med arkaeologen Danmark rundt*. Copenhagen 1963, p. 7.

— *Moesgård*. Aarhus 1970.

KOSSACK, G. 'Zur Geschichte der Urgeschichtsforschung in Schleswig-Holstein'. *Christina Albertina, Kieler Universitäts-Zeitschrift* 2, 1966, p. 51.

LARSEN, SVEND *Et Provinsmuseums Historie. Odense Bys offentlige Samlinger 1860–1935*. Odense 1935.

Ledetraad tie Nordisk Oldkyndighed. see C. J. Thomsen.

LINDQVIST, S. 'Olof Rudbeck d. ä. som fältarkeolog. Rudbeckstudier'. *Festskrift vid Uppsala universitets minnesfest till högtidlighållande av 300-årsminnet av Olof Rudbeck d. ä. födelse*. Uppsala 1930a, p. 249.

— 'Olof Rudbeck d. ä. som arkeolog'. *Uppsala universitets årsskrift* Program 7, 1930b.

LUND, H. 'Akademiet ad Ledreborg'. *Kunstmuseets Årsskrift* LI–LII, 1965, p. 55.

LUND, P. W. 'Om de sydamerikanske Vildes Steenøxer', *Annaler for nordisk Oldkyndighed* 1838–9, p. 159.

LUND, T. 'Danefaelovgivningen og andre regler om fund af sager af historisk vaerdi'. *Juristen* 1942, p. 657.

MACKEPRANG, M. B. *De nordiske Guldbrakteater*. Aarhus 1952.

MAGNUS, OLAUS *Historia de gentibus septentrionalibus*. Rome 1555.

MAGNUSSEN, F. *see* C. J. Thomsen, and C. Molbech.

MALMER, MATS P. *Metodproblem inom järnålderns konsthistoria*. Lund 1963.

MARSTRANDER, Sv. 'Videnskapsselskapets oldsakssamling'. *Årsberetning 1948 for det Kgl. Norske Videnskabers Selskab Museet*, p. 54.

MEINANDER, C. F. 'Ny finsk lag om fornminnen (1963)'. *Tor* 1964, p. 245.

MOBERG, C. A. 'Introduktion till Arkeologi'. *Jämnförande och nordisk fornkunskap*. Stockholm 1969.

MOLBECH, C. Finn Magnussen and G. Forchhammer. *Runamo og Runerne En Committeeberetning til det kgl. danske Videnskabers Selskab*, Copenhagen 1841.

MOLTKE, ERIK *Jon Skonvig og de andre runetegnere* I–II. Copenhagen 1956–8.

'Montelius, O. in memoriam.' Memorial papers by T. J. Arne, S. Reinach, G. Kossinna, H. Kjaer, H. Shetelig, A. Bugge, R. Sernander, H. Olrik, E. Reuterskiöld'. *Nordisk tidskrift* 1922.

MÜLLER, S. 'Mindetale over J. J. A. Worsaae'. *Aarbøger* 1886, p. 1.

— 'Mindre Bidrag til den forhistoriske Archaeologis Methode'. *Aarbøger* 1884, p. 161.

— *Vor Oldtid*. Copenhagen 1897.

— *Nationalmuseet hundrede Aar efter Grundlaeggelsen*. Copenhagen 1907.

'Mindefesten for S. Müller'. *Aarbøger* 1934, p. 1. Memorial tributes by M. Mackeprang, Sune Lindqvist, A. W. Brøgger m. fl.

'Nationalmuseet og Provindsmuseerne' (by F. Ollendorff, Lønborg Friis, F. C. Lorentzen, M. Bidstrup, M. Mackeprang and S. Müller). *Aarbøger* 1912, p. 143.

NEERGAARD, C. 'Thomas Bartholin og Oldforskningen i Danmark i det 17. Aarhundrede'. *Ugeskrift for Laeger* 1916, p. 1836.

NERMAN, B. *Den gotländska fornforskningens historia*. Stockholm 1941.

— 'Oscar Montelius och svenska fornminnesföreningen'. *Fornvännen* 1944, p. 5.

NIELSEN, V. 'Hvilke oldsager er danefae?' *Juristen* 1949, p. 65.

NORDÉN, A. *Kiviksgraven, Svenska fornminnesplatser* 1 (4. uppl.). Stockholm 1942.

NORDMAN, C. A. *Archaeology in Finland before 1920*. Societas Scientiarum Fennica. Helsinki 1968.

NORDMAN, ELIN *Vandring i usynligt rum*. Copenhagen 1960.

OUSAGER, B. 'Danske mindesmaerker om Ole Worm og hans vaerk'. *Skalk* 1960, 3, p. 18.

PETERSEN, CARL S. *Stenalder, Bronzealder, Jernalder. Bidrag til nordisk Arkaeologis Literaerhiistorie 1776–1865*. Copenhagen 1938.

PETERSEN, J. MAGNUS *Minder fra min Virksomhed paa Arkaeologiens Omraade*. Copenhagen 1909.

PETREIUS, NICOLAUS *Cimbrorum et Gothorum origines, migrationes, bella atque coloniae*. Leipzig 1695.

PETRI, OLAVUS 'En Swensk Cröenecka' (ed. J. Sahlgren). *Samlade skrifter af Olavus Petri IV*. Uppsala 1917, p. I and I.

PONTOPPIDAN, E. 'Kort Efterretning om en i Aaret 1744 ved Jaegers-Priis Slott i en Høy funden, saakaldet Jette-Stue. . . .' *Skrifter, som det Kiøbenhavnske Selskab af Laerdoms og Videnskabers Elskere ere fremlagte og oplaeste i Aarene 1743 og 1744*. Copenhagen 1745.

— *Den danske Atlas I*. Copenhagen 1763.

RASMUSSEN, A. *Frederik Münter, Hans Levned og Personlighed*. Copenhagen 1925.

RAUSING, G. *Arkeologien som naturvetenskap*. Lund 1971.

RUDBECK, O. *Atland eller Manheim* I (ed. A. Nelson, Lychnos-Bibliotek 2, 1). Uppsala 1937.

RYDBECK, O. 'Den arkeologiska forskningen och historiska museet vid Lunds universitet under tvåhundra ar 1735–1937'. *Meddelanden från Lunds universitets historiska museum* 1943, p. 165.

Sakses Danesage I–IV (transl. J. Olrik). Copenhagen 1908–12.

SCHEPELERN, H. D. *see* Ole Worm.

SCHÖNBÄCK, B. 'Museet för nordiska fornsaker 100 år'. *Tor* 1958, p. 5.

SCHÜCK, H. *Kgl. Vitterhets, Historie och Antikvitets Akademien* I–VIII. Stockholm 1932–44.

SEHESTED, N. F. B. 'Praktiske Forsøg'. *Archaeologiske Undersøgelser 1878–1881*, p. 3. Copenhagen 1884.

SELLING, D. *Alexander Seton (1768–1828) som fornforskare*. Stockholm 1945.

SHETELIG, H. *Norske museers historie*. Oslo 1944.

SHETELIG, K. 'Haakon Sheteligs utgravninger på Brømlo 1901–42'. *Viking* XXVIII 1964, p. 39.

SJØVOLD, TH. 'Ingvald Undset'. *Viking* 1953, p. 7.

SLOMANN, W. 'Haakon Shetelig'. *Viking* XIX, 1955, p. V.

— 'En antikvarisk-historisk skisse omkring Avaldsnesfunnet'. *Viking* XXVIII, 1964, p. 5.

STEENSTRUP, J. 'Tørvemosernes Bidrag til Kundskab om Landets forhistoriske Natur og Kultur'. *Beretning om Landmandsforsamlingen i Kjøbenhavn 1869*, Copenhagen 1970, p. 336.

STENBERGER, M. 'Tio nordiska arkaeologmöten'. *Tor* 1963, p. 3.

STOBAEUS, K. 'Ceravnii betuliqve lapides dissertatione historica' ill. (1738) *Opera in quibus petrefactorum numismat. et ant. hist.* Dantisci 1753.

SVÄRDSTRÖM E. *Johannes Bureus' arbeten om svenska runinskrifter.* Stockholm 1936.

SVENNUNG, J. 'Zur Geschichte des Goticismus'. *Skrifter utg. av K. hum. vetenskapssamfundet i Uppsala* 44, 2 B, Stockholm 1967.

Swedish Archaeological Bibliography 1939–48. Uppsala 1951.

SYV, P. *200 Viser om Konger, Kemper oc Andre (1695).* Copenhagen 1787.

SØRENSEN, W. *Fromme Sjaeles gode Gjerninger.* Copenhagen 1809.

TALLGREN, A. M. 'Geschichte der antiquarischen Forschung in Finland', *Eurasia Septemtrionalis Antiqua* X, 1936, p. 199.

THOMSEN, C. J. 'Kortfattet Udsigt over Mindesmaerker og Oldsager fra Nordens Fortid'. *Ledetraad til Nordisk Oldkyndighed.* Copenhagen 1836, p. 27.

THOMSEN, C. J. and F. MAGNUSSEN 'Efterretninger om Monumenterne ved Jellinge, samt de i Aarene 1820 og 1821 der foretagne Undersøgelser'. *Antiqvariske Annaler* 4, 1827, p. 64.

THORDEMAN, B. 'Skattfyndsregalet i Sverige och Danmark'. *Fornvännen* 1945, p. 189.

THORVILDSEN, ELISE 'Dyssen ved Daempegården i Tokkekøb Hegn'. *Kultur og folkeminder* 1965, p. 3.

THORVILDSEN, K. 'Grønhøj ved Horsens'. *Aarbøger* 1946, p. 73.

UNDSET, I. *Fra Akershus til Akropolis.* Christiania and Copenhagen 1892.

VEDEL, E. *Af mit Livs Historie.* Copenhagen 1906.

WANDALL, P. T. *De paa Jaegerspriis ved Mindesteene haedrede Fortiente Maends Levnets-Beskrivelser* I.

Copenhagen 1783.

WERLAUFF, E. C. *Erindringer om Guldhornstyveriet.* Copenhagen 1858.

WORM, O. *De aureo cornu.* Copenhagen 1641.

— *Danicorum Monumentorum libri sex.* Copenhagen 1643.

— *Museum Wormianum seu Historia rerum rariorum.* Amsterdam 1655.

— *Breve fra og til*, I–III, Copenhagen 1965–8. (Ed. and translated into Danish by H. D. Schlepelern).

WORSAAE, J. A. A. *Danmarks Oldtid oplyst ved Oldsager og Gravhøie.* Copenhagen 1843. English ed. *The Primeval Antiquities of Denmark*, London 1849.

— *Runamo og Braavalleslaget. Et Bidrag til archaeologisk Kritik.* Copenhagen 1844 (Add. Copenhagen 1845).

— 'Fund af romerske Oldsager i Danmark'. *Annaler for nordisk Oldkyndighed*, 1849, p. 390.

— *Afbildninger fra Det Kongelige Museum for Nordiske Oldsager i Kjøbenhavn.* Copenhagen 1854.

— (on the stone age of the 'kitchen middens'). *Oversigt for møder i Videnskabernes selskab* 1859, p. 93.

— 'Conferentsraaderne C. C. Rafns og C. J. Thomsens Fortjenester af Oldskriftselskabet og af Oldtidsvidenskaben i det Hele'. *Aarbøger* 1866, p. 3.

— 'Om Opdagelsen af Den aeldre Jernalder. Bemaerkninger til C. F. Herbst's Beskrivelse af "Varpelev-Fundet"'. *Aarbøger* 1866, 1867, p. 1.

— 'Ruslands og det skandinaviske Nordens Bebyggelse og aeldste Kulturforhold'. *Aarbøger* 1872, p. 309.

— 'Om Bevaringen af de faedrelandske Oldsager og Mindesmaerker i Danmark'. *Aarbøger* 1877.

— *Breve 1840–1885*, (ed. Ad. Clement). Copenhagen 1930.

— *En Oldgrandskers Erindringer* (ed. V. Hermansen). Copenhagen 1934.

— *Af en Oldgrandskers Breve'* (ed. V. Hermansen). Copenhagen 1938.

ÅBERG, N. 'Oscar Montelius som forskare', *Kgl. vitterhets, historie och antikvitetsakadamiens handlingar* 57, 1943, intro.

ØRSNES, M. Preface to C. Engelhardt's *Sønderjyske og fynske mosefund* I, 1969, p. V.

Index